UNAFRAID

UNAFRAID

STARING DOWN TERROR
AS A NAVY SEAL
AND SINGLE DAD

EDDIE PENNEY
AND KEITH WOOD

UNAFRAID

UNAFRAID
Staring Down Terror as a Navy SEAL and Single Dad

ISBN 978-1-5445-3288-2 *Hardcover*
      978-1-5445-3289-9 *Paperback*
      978-1-5445-3290-5 *Ebook*
      978-1-5445-3291-2 *Audiobook*

To my family, friends, and mentors, all of whom shaped who I am. And to the next generation of warriors who will stand between good and evil.

CONTENTS

AUTHOR'S NOTE

In the special operations community, we follow most training events and real-world operations with an after-action review, better known as a "hot wash." A hot wash is a no-holds-barred dissection of the event, highlighting what went right and, more importantly, what went wrong. The concept is that, in order to improve and grow, we have to be 100 percent honest about our strengths and weaknesses. If you suck, you need to know it so that you can get better. This brutal honesty saves lives and creates more effective warriors.

At the end of each chapter is a hot wash on my life. I look back and comment on the lessons learned by those events with the benefit of hindsight. Those paragraphs are directed toward my children, my friends, and anyone out there reading or listening to this book, regardless of their career path or circumstances. Let my failures be your lessons.

Due to the sensitive operational information that I was privy to during most of my military career, there are parts of my life that

I simply cannot talk about. As part of my ongoing commitment to our nation, our military, and the men and women who serve, I have taken great pains to ensure that no classified information or terminology is used in *Unafraid*. To that end, this manuscript was submitted to the Department of Defense for pre-publication review. DOD approved it "as amended," changing some minor terminology and redacting a few lines.

I'd like to pause here and humbly say "thank you" to every man and woman in the armed forces. Though the special operations community gets a lot of attention, we are but one piece of the puzzle. Every single job is extremely important and necessary to make the military machine work. I am in debt to the very many service members, and their families, who made a lasting impression on me. For many of them, the fight continues. To me, you are all selfless heroes.

As I write these words, Afghanistan is in chaos. The land that my brothers and sisters fought and died for has been turned over to the same terrorists who harbored the architects of 9/11. Individual Afghans who stood up to fight for their country's freedom on the promise that we would never abandon them are being left, along with their families, to be tortured and killed by the Taliban. As an American, I am embarrassed.

More than twenty-three hundred US troops were killed during that two-decade conflict, along with nearly five thousand US contractors. Tens of thousands of soldiers, sailors, airmen, and Marines were left with horrific wounds—some visible, some not. My closest friends can be found in the hallowed ground of Arlington National Cemetery.

Was the sacrifice worth it? I believe so. When I think about the generation of Afghans that grew up under the blanket of protection that US and coalition forces provided, I see hope. Young women who would have spent their lives wearing burqas and forced into illiteracy under Taliban rule are now college graduates. Boys who would have been forced into duty as fighters for the regime or a warlord instead enjoyed relative normalcy. An entire generation of Afghans tasted freedom from tyranny, and maybe, just maybe, they will fight to preserve it.

Eddie Penney
Texas, USA, August 2021

SEPTEMBER 2009

Our home in Virginia Beach was a mess. I returned from a training trip to find our house all but empty. When she left, my wife, Leia, had taken everything except the trash she'd left strewn about: coat hangers, a plastic laundry basket, an empty lipstick container, and a soda straw. The odds and ends of life, scattered in the haste of breaking up our family. She'd given keys to our home to friends who had then come and gone as they pleased, taking my belongings and leaving empty liquor bottles and food containers behind.

I went to work cleaning up the house and preparing it for sale; it was too far from work, and there were too many bad memories there. I had not seen or heard from my three young children since Leia had left with them weeks earlier, and I was beginning to worry about their well-being. After so many deployments I was accustomed to not seeing them, but this was different. Leia's mental health and substance abuse issues had escalated into extremely volatile behavior and repeated attempts at suicide. I had tried my best to stay in the marriage for the sake of my kids, but it just wasn't going to work out for us.

I was well into my career as a Navy SEAL, an assaulter and breacher assigned to one of the most elite special operations units in existence ███████████████████████. Our teams are required to be immediately available when they are a part of the designated alert unit. If we get the call, we have to get to the compound immediately and prepare to respond to a real-world crisis. We were in the late stages of our training cycle, which meant that it was our turn to be on alert for deployment. Our gear was packed and ready for any contingency that might arise.

I was painting the living room walls when the call came. I put the lid on the paint can, dropped the brush, grabbed my keys, and raced to work. Alongside my teammates, with my hands and hair still dotted with paint, I loaded my gear and boarded an Air Force transport aircraft.

We taxied without fanfare, and were soon over the dark waters of the Atlantic. Most of the guys swallowed sleeping tablets and found places to stretch out on the aircraft's aluminum deck or nylon-webbed seats. I built my own little nest alongside a pallet of gear, but sleep would not come.

My thoughts drifted again to my children Kailha, Samantha, and Triston. I wondered where they were and what they were doing. They didn't ask for any of this. It wasn't their fault that the family was so unstable, or that I was gone for months at a time on some of the most dangerous missions imaginable. They knew that many of Daddy's friends had never come home, and that had to weigh on them. Would this be the operation where the odds finally caught up with me? Triston was only a few months old and would never remember me. For some reason that bothered me more than dying. Eventually, I drifted off to sleep.

Hours later we were on a ship off the coast of the Horn of Africa, preparing for a direct-action mission on a high-value terrorist target. These are the violent and often lethal battles that the public rarely hears about unless something goes wrong. This time it was different: our target was a senior al-Qaeda leader, who had been on the run for years. His name was one of the ten on the FBI's Most Wanted Terrorists List due to his alleged involvement in the 1998 US Embassy bombings, which killed 224 people and injured more than 4,000. Needless to say, his death made the news.

FOUNDATIONS

I am very much a child of the 1980s. I was born in 1978 and spent my childhood in the suburbs just outside of Cincinnati, Ohio. Cincinnati lies in the extreme southwest portion of the state, just north of the Ohio River. The river marks the Ohio-Kentucky state line, making Cincinnati a city where the South meets the Midwest, with strong influences of both regional cultures.

I grew up as the only child of two parents who were scratching out a middle-class existence as best they could. My dad did drywall as well as other contracting jobs, and worked long hours. When he wasn't working, he was usually out playing sports—bowling during the week and softball on the weekends. I'd watch him play softball on Friday and Saturday nights, and he quickly became my own larger-than-life personal hero. He was a great guy, but I don't think I'm being unfair when I say that his priorities were not at home in those years. His tendency to stay away from the house as often as possible spelled trouble for my parents' marriage, and that absence, combined with his frequent alcohol use, led my parents to divorce when I was seven.

My mom did clerical work downtown, mostly payroll, and she took some accounting courses that she always seemed to be studying for. Neither of my parents had a college degree. The divorce was more or less amicable: she had primary custody, and I was able to see my dad on weekends and the occasional school night. Mom got the house, and that is where we lived until I was in the sixth grade. Our home was a small split-level, three-bedroom house with a one-car garage on a packed suburban street. It was one of dozens upon dozens of nearly identical houses, each on its own quarter-acre slice of paradise. I could walk out of my door and have instant access to dozens of other kids my own age.

I was all boy. When I wasn't in school or asleep, I could be found jumping fences, running around the neighborhood, and generally trespassing on other peoples' property. Bodies of water were my favorite haunts, and I spent hours walking the creeks, looking for snakes or other creatures. I played in the woods, built forts with my friends, and fished and swam in local ponds. Since the Ohio Valley is filled with rolling hills and trees, it was a huge playground, and I took full advantage.

Our neighborhood was in Anderson Township, a riverfront community fifteen minutes east of downtown Cincinnati. Anderson was, and still is, a mixture of housing developments, wooded areas, and farmland. It was lush and green and very Middle America. Mine was a working-class neighborhood: cops, firefighters, teachers, plumbers, and administrative workers like my mother—the people who go to work, pay their taxes, and raise their kids to have a better life than the one that they worked hard to build. The kinds of people who fight the wars and work in the factories. It was a community I am proud to be from. Things weren't always perfect, but from my perspective, it was a pretty idyllic time and place in which to grow up.

It started early, flexing in my Underoos circa 1982.

I was a happy kid, but often found myself in trouble. I spent most of my grade school summers in day camp at the local rec center. We would play sports like kickball and tennis, do arts and crafts, and swim for hours. I had a great time, and the all-day schedule allowed my mom to maintain her obligations at work. One day at camp found us a few hundred yards from the rec center, playing in the woods around a Catholic school. To a nine-year-old kid, it was a massive campus; I can still picture the stately main building with its tall white pillars towering above us. We were hiding in the bushes when we spotted a free-standing fire alarm, similar to the call boxes that we now see on college campuses. There was a glass door that had to be pulled down along with a lever inside. Part of me really wanted to pull that handle to see what would happen, but I was scared of getting into trouble. But with the other kids double-daring me, I decided that it would be a really good idea to give it a try. I approached the call box cautiously, like it was a wild animal. I peeked back at the other boys for encouragement before pulling down the glass door. To my relief, nothing happened. In for a penny, in for a pound. I pulled down the lever inside and immediately heard a faint bell ringing in the distance, the kind that you would find in an old fire house. The wail of fire trucks' sirens came next, the engines speeding toward us. Terrified, I ran into the woods and hid.

One of the firefighters jumped off the truck and approached our camp counselor to see what the emergency was. My friends ratted me out immediately and I walked out of my hiding spot with my head down. A big, strong fireman stood there with his yellow raincoat, heavy boots, and numbered red fire hat. He wasn't smiling. I wanted to crawl inside a hole and wait for my mommy. The firefighter read me the riot act, explaining that him being there on a false alarm could prevent him from responding to a real emergency. It was a very brief but memorable education.

The camp staff told my parents what had happened, and, in hindsight, my mother responded in the best way possible. Mom made me sit down and write a two-page letter to the fire house, apologizing for what I'd done and communicating my appreciation for the role that they played in our community. Not only did she ensure that I would never do anything like this again, she instilled in me the value of public servants in our society. That Saturday morning, my mom drove me to the fire house so that I could hand-deliver the letter. The firefighter who had lectured me happened to be there, and I handed him the letter. He read it, and you could tell that he was genuinely moved by it. He was incredibly nice about the whole thing. My mom's good parenting ensured that I actually learned something from the experience, rather than merely being punished for it. Well done, Mom.

One day when I was nine years old, I saw a moving truck unloading into the house across the street from mine, and hoped that the family would have a boy my own age. As it turned out, they did. His name was Ozgur, but he quickly became known as "Oz." He and his family had emigrated directly from Turkey but, as it turned out, they fit in pretty seamlessly in our working-class neighborhood. Oz's dad was a woodworker and his mom stayed home to raise the children. In later years, I wondered what religion they'd practiced; I learned later that they had not been of any specific affiliation. Oz's father was very thankful for the generosity displayed by Christian families during the transition to the US, though, and has a fondness and respect for that faith that has endured through the years.

I met Oz the day after these neighbors arrived, when I watched a little boy who was clearly of Middle Eastern descent walk sheepishly toward the bus stop. He was a new kid, in a new school, in a new country—I'm sure he felt very alone and out of place. I've always been competitive—I had the reputation as the fastest boy on the street, and I would challenge any newcomers to a race to maintain my title. Like an animal that sees a rival, I felt my adrenaline surge as Oz appeared. I immediately asked him to race. I was sure that I would win; I'd beaten everyone up to that point, and this guy was from Turkey, wherever that was. We had a standard racecourse that ran from a telephone pole to a stop sign on the corner. It seemed like a long distance at that age but, truthfully, it was probably only twenty-five yards. Another kid stood at the finish line and dropped his hands to signal the start of the race. We came off the line in unison, our feet pounding the sidewalk. I was on the left side and I watched helplessly as Oz pulled away ahead of me. It was over in a few seconds and the new kid, who immediately became one of my closest friends, won the race and the title. He was so fast that I am sure that he kept that crown until he moved away from the neighborhood.

An early lesson for me was that, no matter how good you are (or think you are) at something, there is someone out there who is better. Surrounding yourself with those people raises the bar. I remember once hearing, **"If you want to be a lion, then hang out with lions, not sheep."** I have learned that this is one of life's most important truths: you are who you surround yourself with.

Other than playing the video game *Contra* on Nintendo from time to time, I don't recall playing indoors much as a kid. Speaking of *Contra*, if you don't know the cheat code (↑ ↑ ↓ ↓ ← → ← → B A start), you're likely either a millennial or a Communist.

Oz and I were pretty well inseparable, thanks to a shared love of the outdoors. We called ourselves "the snake killers," and we would walk for hours in search of prey. We would make spears, bows, and arrows, or any other weapon that would protect us in our little fantasyland and, of course, kill any snake that we saw. The two of us fished a lot and, on occasion, put firecrackers in the mouths of fish that we caught. In hindsight, I may not have been 100 percent truthful when I answered the question about "torturing small animals" during my military psych evaluation, but it was all done out of boyhood curiosity, not a sadistic desire to cause harm.

Oz was rail skinny and his mother was always trying to put weight on him. Every hour, on the hour, she would call out for him, he would sprint home, chug an entire glass of milk, and sprint back to wherever we happened to be playing.

With Oz at my side, my adventures became even more exciting. One of our favorite activities was something that we called the "jungle run." We would start at the top of a very steep hill and run down at full speed. Since there were random rocks, stumps, roots, and other debris you would find on the forest floor, it made a great natural obstacle course. How we never got seriously hurt, I'll never know. It is a time that I will always remember and cherish and, little did I know then, it was grooming me for my future by lighting the warrior's flame within me.

On one memorable day, Oz and I decided that we wanted to go spearfishing. The only problem was that we didn't have any spears. Undeterred, we broke the heads off a pair of brooms so that all that remained were the wooden shafts. *I am sure my mom won't mind*, I thought. After all, it was for a good cause. For the spearheads, we taped nails and screws onto the ends—what could go wrong? Like all good hunters, we had to practice before the big hunt. We walked down the street from my house and into the woods. Looking back, I can imagine our neighbors were probably wondering what we were up to as we walked by, wielding these medieval-looking weapons. A good-sized tree made for an attractive target, and we took turns heaving our homemade spears toward the trunk. I went first: I sized up the tree, picturing it as one of those big fish that we were going after. I closed my nondominant eye and threw the shaft with all of my strength. My aim was perfect and I knew it was going to hit my mark. Instead of the spear lodging itself into the tree the way I'd imagined, though, it bounced harmlessly onto the forest floor. Talk about a bummer.

I picked up my spear and moved to the side of the tree so Oz could take his turn. Oz grasped his weapon, got into his attack position, and let it soar through the air. It was a beautiful sight. It had perfect trajectory and was headed directly toward the tree—I had no doubt that this was going to stick. I was wrong. As the tip of the spear hit the tree, it bounced off at a sharp angle and headed right for me. All of a sudden, I was directly in the path of this crude weapon. As I stood, paralyzed by shock and fear, the spear finally reached me and stuck in my ankle near my Achilles tendon. (At least we finally got it to stick in something.) Oz and I just stared at one another in disbelief. I didn't scream out or cry; I was too shocked. Oz's eyes would meet mine; we would both look down at my leg and then back up. There we were, out in the woods, away from everyone, with a spear sticking out of my leg, with a screw embedded at least halfway through my flesh.

We made the decision to make our way out of the forest and back toward my house to get some help and face the inevitable punishment from my mom. Oz did his best to hold the spear in my leg while I walked, resting most of my weight on my good leg and Oz. The pace was slow and painful, but we eventually made our way out of the woods and back onto our street. As crazy as this sounds, I remember telling myself that I might need to endure pain like this in the future to survive in combat, and those thoughts drove me further, despite the agony. Finally, though, I couldn't take the pain anymore, and I knew that the spear had to come out if I was going to make it home. There was no great way to do this so I said to Oz, "You need to pull this out of my leg."

We stood on the sidewalk and, after a brief moment of that comment processing in Oz's brain, he simply grabbed the spear and started yanking. The nail was poking the back of my leg without penetrating it, but the screw was deeply embedded into my flesh and did what it was designed to do by resisting the attempted removal. Each time Oz pulled, I could see the threads of the screw slipping out from under my skin, little by little. You could hear each thread of the screw pop as Oz pulled and, finally, it cleared my leg. I took a few tentative steps and, with each movement, blood and muscle tissue squirted from the entry wound. I don't think that I ever cried that day but, without a doubt, that walk was one of the most painful moments of my rough-and-tumble childhood. When we finally made it to my house, my mom got the shock of her life. I ended up spending four days in the hospital recovering; so much for our spearfishing trip. Lesson learned, sort of.

I didn't have any siblings, but I did have other family in the area. Our extended family usually rented a houseboat once a year, where I would spend time with my aunt, uncle, cousins, and my parents. (Even though they were divorced, they maintained a cordial relationship so that my childhood would be as normal as possible.) We'd find a cove, swim during the day, and fish at dawn and dusk. One of my favorite things to do during those trips was to grab the fishing line and dive as deep as I could, often to the bottom of the lake or river. I would place the baited hooks in strategic locations where I thought we were likely to catch fish, before swimming back to the surface, my lungs screaming for air. If we snagged a line on some unseen obstacle, I would put on my dive mask and swim down to free it—sometimes with fish attached to it. I guess I was always destined to be a frogman.

During one of those trips to Tennessee, something happened that left an indelible impression on me. We were headed out in a small motorboat that came with the houseboat rental. The small craft was easy to maneuver, so it was what we used to fish and explore the lake. We had just climbed in and were headed out for the day when an unsecured anchor fell overboard. Without hesitation, my dad just jumped into the water headfirst, diving down to the lake bottom to recover the lost anchor. A few seconds later he broke the surface, anchor in hand. He slung it into the bottom of the boat and climbed back in as if nothing had happened. **There was no talk, no discussion, he just got it done**. It may not seem like much, but at my young age it blew me away. It stirred something inside me, right then and there; **if there's something that needs to be handled, you handle it. Period**. [When we were writing this book, I mentioned to my dad that I was using that story as an example. He had no clue what I was talking about. I had to remind him that he'd done it.]

As you may have guessed by now, I wasn't exactly an easy kid to manage. I meant well, but my adventures often put me at odds with my mom's rules. We moved into our new house during junior high, and the architect must not have had any sons. There was a second-floor balcony that overlooked the living room—and it just so happened to be placed directly over the white L-shaped sectional couch that my mom loved. One of my favorite tricks was to drop my cat, Alex (named after Jean-Claude Van Damme's character in the movie *Double Impact*), over the railing and watch him bounce safely off the couch cushions. I would repeat the process until I got bored, which usually took some time. I'm pretty sure Alex hated me, but he endured this all without injury. Sooner or later, the temptation to try it myself became too much. "If the cat can do it, why can't I?" I started by dangling myself over the railing and dropping onto the couch below feetfirst. Soon I was upping the ante, jumping off the balcony and landing on my back or bottom. My mom couldn't figure out why her beloved couch was broken, or why there were streaks on the wall below the balcony, until my aunt came over one day and put the pieces together. She was a sharp woman and quickly figured out what was going on.

"Eddie, do you know anything about this?" she asked. I resisted at first, but finally admitted to going over the balcony "once or twice." My mom flipped out, understandably.

Soon after, I was doing some of my first experiments with indoor explosives, something that I became extremely proficient in years later. It didn't go as well the first time, though. I knew that I wanted to be an Explosive Ordnance Disposal (EOD) expert, a job in the military that requires bravely defusing bombs just in the nick of time. As practice, I lit the wick on a strip of Black Cat firecrackers, thinking that I could stop the flame before it caused the fireworks to detonate. Needless to say, that didn't go as planned.

I dove for cover as dozens of firecrackers went off in the small upstairs hallway, sounding a lot like a long burst of machine gun fire. My ears were ringing, the hallway filled with smoke, and the carpet burst into flames. I managed not to burn the house down, but my mom wasn't too happy with what I'd done to the flooring in the new home that she'd worked so hard for.

It didn't end there. When I was home alone, I'd often practice Close Quarters Battle inside the house. I really had no clue what CQB was—I just wanted to look cool like the guys in the movies. What I lacked in expertise I made up for in enthusiasm. I would clear the house of imaginary bad guys with my paintball gun, shooting various items that I knew that I could clean up—toasters, the tiled fireplace mantel, you name it. My efforts to clean up weren't always effective and, of course, Mom found out. She did her best to deal out an appropriate punishment, though I can't recall exactly what that was. I'd like to say that I grew out of being a troublemaker, but the truth is, I just found another direction.

Though I didn't grow up in a particularly religious household, my mother took me to church a few times as a kid. I'm not sure whether it was a Presbyterian or Baptist congregation, but it was some brand of Protestant Christianity. I mostly remember that when they handed out vanilla wafers to the kids in Sunday School, they gave me an apple instead to keep me from bouncing off the walls. I guess a hyperactive future commando on a sugar high wasn't exactly helping them maintain control of the class. If they taught me anything back then, it certainly didn't stick with me.

Frankly, this part may sound like BS, but if you want to believe the war stories in the upcoming chapters, you've got to believe this one as well. It was not long after my parents' divorce and we were still living in our first house, where my bedroom was right next to my mother's. I was sound asleep in my twin bed one night when something woke me up. I shot up in bed like someone in a horror movie and slowly turned my head. As I did, in the darkness, I saw a man in my room. I immediately knew that the man was Jesus. He had the beard that he's always portrayed with, and he wore flowing white robes. His face was flawless and his long brown hair tumbled down his shoulders as it would in a Rembrandt painting.

Though I was startled, I wasn't scared. In fact, I felt an absolute sense of peace and serenity. He didn't move or say anything, he just stood there looking at me peacefully. I could see the bookshelf behind him, so he was slightly transparent, almost like a hologram. His figure illuminated the room in a soft glow. I tried to say something but the words wouldn't come out of me. I just sat there staring.

After a few moments he simply vanished as if he'd turned into vapor, leaving the room suddenly pitch dark. An overwhelming fear came over me. I wanted to sprint to my mom's room, but I was too terrified to move. I tried to call out, but the most that I could muster was a soft "M-m-mom." Eventually, I built up the courage to get up and run out the door. I crawled into my mom's bed, still shaking. I never told her what had just happened; I think I mumbled something about "seeing something." I tossed and turned next to her for hours, too scared to sleep.

I know what you're thinking: that I had a very vivid dream. I can't prove that it wasn't but, in my heart, I know what I saw and know that I was awake when I saw it. If you're rolling your eyes at this point, stick with me. I spent the rest of the day thinking about what I'd seen in my room, nervous about the prospect of sleeping there again. My childhood logic came up with a solution: I would sleep with a blanket over my head. What I couldn't see, couldn't hurt me, right? It must have been summertime, since I remember sweating heavily under the blanket, but that didn't stop me from keeping myself covered up. Just for good measure, I slept with a night light on.

A few nights later I'd returned to some semblance of normalcy and was, once again, in a deep sleep. I awakened to the sound of soft organ music, the kind that you'd hear before a church service or wedding. You may think that organ music is peaceful but, to me, it just sounded creepy. Then I heard the distinct sound of children giggling. My arm had found its way out of my protective blanket during the night and I felt a tickling sensation in my armpit. For the second time that week, I was terrified. Paralyzed with fear, I was finally able to call out to my mother and everything stopped. Once again, I found myself in her bed, sleepless for the rest of the night.

I continued to sleep restlessly for the next few nights but my visitors never returned. I made a vow to myself that I wanted nothing to do with religion, that I would never again go to church. I wasn't agnostic—I was terrified. I began having recurring nightmares in which Jesus would burst into my house like, well, a Navy SEAL, and take me away from my mother. He may have been the world's savior, but to me he was the boogeyman. It would be many years before those feelings of fear would subside.

In seventh grade I changed schools and was excited to make a new friend, a kid my age named Forrest. He asked me to sleep over at his house one weekend and I was pumped about it. What I didn't know when I accepted the invitation was that his father was a pastor in a local church. Another one of those crazy Christians.

When I walked into his house, one of the first things that I noticed was a painting of Jesus on the wall. I freaked out. I ran to the phone, called my mom, and asked her to pick me up. There was no way that I was going to sleep in that house.

My aversion to religion stuck with me into adulthood. Sure, I went to plenty of weddings and funerals, but I never attended regular services. And yes, I prayed to God on more than one helicopter ride, but "please don't let me die tonight" is hardly a deep dive into Christianity.

As I grew older, sports took over my life, and I was able to channel some of that endless energy into a positive outlet. There was something about playing competitive sports that appealed to me in a fundamental way. In hindsight, it was probably the process of learning about winning and losing, as well as the realization of what it takes to work hard to get better at something. Nothing worthwhile comes easy. I played football, baseball, soccer, and volleyball in the summer, and made a pretty unsuccessful attempt at becoming a basketball player.

My little league baseball coach, Mr. Murphy, was the ideal role model, both for a coach and a man. He was a Vietnam veteran as well as a police officer, and he loved to lift weights. He had a gym in his basement, and his son, Little Murph, and I would often sneak down just to watch him throw around iron. Just like that, a seed was planted. Working out would be part of my life. He was an intimidating figure whose gaze would keep you in check just about 100 percent of the time. Watching him coach our team, seeing the way he treated people, and noticing how he stayed in top physical shape was inspirational to me. He was an amazing man who positively influenced people wherever he went. I wanted to be just like him. **This is a prime example of how you just never know who is watching you; you just may inspire someone with your words and actions.**

Later, my sporting interests evolved to meet reality. During my freshman year of high school, I showed up for football practice and was shocked at the size of some of my fellow players. I was in need of a growth spurt. These guys were a lot heavier than I was, and they towered over me. I called my dad and told him, "I'm not doing this; these guys are huge." So, I quit.

The following day, a friend recommended that I try the swim team. I resisted at first, making a crack about the tiny Speedo swimsuits that the team wore. He was persistent, though, and I agreed to give it a try. I called my mom to let her know that I wouldn't be coming home after school, and headed to the swimming pool.

The first thing that the coach asked me to do was to swim a single pool length. I'd spent my summers swimming in ponds and lakes—how could this be any different? I jumped in, swam the twenty-five-yard length of the pool, and felt like I was going to die—my muscles ached and my lungs starved for oxygen. It was a very humbling experience, but the physical and mental challenge of the sport hooked me immediately. Before long, my body adjusted to the cardiovascular load and I gravitated toward distance events in both freestyle and backstroke.

I swam year-round, both at school and at the local YMCA, and my coach became one of the greatest influences in my life. Larry Lyons was in his fifties at the time, but he was a total stud—known locally as "Mr. Swim." He was a tremendous motivator who understood the sport well and always knew what to say to make you perform. Coach Lyons was hard on us in the right way, when we needed it, not to tear us down but to build us up and inspire us to do greater things. He was the kind of coach who made us want to work harder to impress him and to better ourselves. Before long, I found myself swimming as much for him as I did for me. I respected him and wanted desperately to earn his respect in kind. He was a great mentor and leader, and he brought the best out of all of us. One particular thing he would always say that has stuck with me is, **"Take care of the little things, and the big things will take care of themselves."** Like Coach Murphy, Coach Lyons was a motivator—something that I aspired to be.

Life was good: I was competitive in a sport that I loved, I had a good group of friends around me, and I was on the path to fulfill my dream of serving in the military. Then, in May of 1995, Coach Lyons, who had inspired and driven me to be my very best, died of a heart attack during a canoe trip. I had never lost anyone close to me other than grandparents before, and I was stunned. Nearly every swimmer in the Cincinnati area came out for his funeral—he was that well-loved.

After his death, I showed up for swim practice and began my workout, but without Coach Lyons, my motivation was gone. I knew right then and there that my swimming career was over. I left practice that day and never returned; my heart just wasn't in it. Instead of swimming my senior year, I focused on preparing for my upcoming military career. As I look back on this decision, as hard as it was, I believe it was the right choice for me.

I have always wanted to serve in the Armed Forces. I can actually remember the exact moment when I knew for sure that a military career was my calling. My mother took me to a Cincinnati Reds game in the early 1990s, during the Gulf War. I remember seeing the patriotic bumper stickers adorned with eagles and American flags that read "Support Our Troops" pretty much everywhere that I looked. I felt such pride seeing these symbols of freedom and recognizing how people supported the troops deploying overseas. Everyone was on their team. After hearing horror stories from veterans of the Vietnam era, it was a breath of fresh air.

It was a night game and, of course, at the beginning they played "The Star-Spangled Banner." Everyone proudly stood up and, as the song began, the TV screens around the stadium displayed messages like "God bless America and the troops fighting for our freedom back here in the USA." As the song ended, a formation of military fighter jets flew over the stadium—the roar of their engines' afterburners was surpassed only by the roar of the crowd. **I felt a warmth of pride and patriotism come over my body that was something I had never felt before, and it was beautiful**. I did not know exactly what I wanted to do in the military, but I knew I wanted to serve this amazing country and its citizens. From that night on, I was on a mission to protect the United States of America.

As time progressed, I fell deeper in love with all things military and desperately wanted to be the best of the best. I soon learned from watching every Sylvester Stallone, Chuck Norris, Jean Claude Van Damme, and Arnold Schwarzenegger film that special operations was the place to be.

And then something happened that sealed (pun intended) my fate: I watched a movie titled *Navy SEALs*, starring Charlie Sheen and Michael Biehn. The film covered a team of SEALs as they chased and fought terrorists across the globe. These black-clad commandos crashed through skylights with submachineguns blazing and jumped out of a C-130 36,000 feet over the ocean. They fought bravely and ferociously, and partied just as hard. I was glued to the TV and would pause and then rewind just so that I could get a closer look at what gear they were wearing. You can never start too early, I thought, and I wanted to put my own kit together just like theirs. As an impressionable teenager, I was amazed how they took down the bad guys with such style and made it look so easy. I don't know whether it cost the Navy anything to assist in the production of that film, but I can say that it was the mother of all recruitment tools for the SEAL Teams, and worth every penny that may have been spent on it.

For most of my teenage years, I lived and breathed wanting to be a Navy SEAL. At night, I would sneak around the neighborhood, practicing my surveillance techniques and seeing what I could find out about nearby homes. In hindsight, I'm lucky that I didn't get arrested for being a Peeping Tom, but my motives were innocent: I just wanted to start my training as soon as possible.

During the fall of my senior year, I had to wait after school one day for my ride home, and so, as soon as my classes let out, I walked to the grocery store nearby. I walked around browsing, killing time. I went to the magazine section to check out what was new, and what I found was the November 1995 issue of *Popular Mechanics* magazine. That issue had a feature article titled "Weapons and Tactics of the Navy SEALS," complete with photos and detailed descriptions of their weapons, vehicles, and equipment. The cover featured a SEAL in dive gear, kneeling in the surf with an MP5 submachine gun at the ready. It was as if they had created the entire article specifically for me. I had to have it, but when I looked into my wallet I discovered that I didn't have enough money. I was disappointed and started to read it repeatedly to memorize as much of the information as I could. I finally decided that I *had* to have it—and so I stole it, something that I had never done before. I felt tremendous guilt afterward and have never stolen anything since that day.

I was on a direct path to the SEAL Teams, or so I thought. A close friend that I knew from swimming had been a year ahead of me and, after high school, had joined the Marine Corps. As his graduation from basic training at Parris Island was drawing near, I got a call from his younger brother, asking if I wanted to go down for the ceremony. I was excited at the prospect of seeing my friend and congratulating him in person on his accomplishment of making it through boot camp, so I accepted the invitation.

Arriving at Parris Island on the South Carolina coast, I got to see the obstacle courses that the recruits had to navigate, the parade grounds on which they drilled, and the barracks building where they lived. I was in awe of the entire scene. During the graduation ceremony, I watched as hundreds of new Marines marched in perfect unison, their impeccable uniforms moving as one. Whoever designed the Marine Corps uniforms was probably the single greatest recruiter of all time. The tradition and pageantry of the event was simply too much for a seventeen-year-old to take and, by the end, I'd decided that I was going to be a Marine. My career as a Navy SEAL would have to wait.

Halfway through my senior year, I visited the Marine Corps recruiter. Each job in the military has a Military Occupational Specialty, or MOS. The backbone MOS of the Marine Corps is 0311, Infantry Rifleman—the guys that hit the beaches and storm out of helicopters. I proudly signed on the line and sealed my fate.

There was nothing I wanted to do more than to be the guy on the front lines if our country had to go to war. Since I was only seventeen, I had to have both my mom and dad sign for me in order to enlist. They were a bit reluctant, but stood by my decision and gave Uncle Sam their blessing. As soon as I graduated from high school, I would be headed to Parris Island and would proudly wear the uniform.

I was so excited about my enlistment that I told all my friends at school about it, and tried to persuade some of them to join with me. One good friend fell for my pitch and enlisted, as well. We ended up joining under what they called the "buddy program," which assigned paired friends to the same boot camp class. This sounded like a great idea; we were both happy that we would not be alone on what would be the toughest journey of our lives up to that point.

My last day as a civilian, August 1996. I had no idea what was in store for me.

After high school graduation and a final carefree summer with my friends, it was time to make my lifelong dream a reality. August 23, 1996, came around quickly and off to boot camp we went. The first stop was to MEPS, the Military Entrance Processing Station, where recruits are introduced to some of the best red tape that the US government has to offer. Of course, there was a problem with my paperwork and my transition to Basic Training was delayed by a day. My friend went ahead to Parris Island while I waited impatiently for things to clear. They promised that we would be linked up again once my records were good to go, but it never happened. I later discovered that he had hurt his knee and was being discharged. My friend would soon be on his way back to Cincinnati; and I was all alone with the other scared recruits. I was sad to find out that he was leaving; the comfort of enduring the training alongside someone that I knew and trusted was over. Looking back, his departure was my first class in mental toughness.

HOT WASH

Your childhood shapes who you are, but it doesn't have to define you. Making mistakes as a child will make you a better adult. I respect my mother for the way that she disciplined me, always encouraging me to do the right thing. I hated her for it at the time, but taking that letter to the firehouse taught me that my actions had consequences and instilled in me a lasting respect for public service. **Life is an endless series of choices—moral and ethical crossroads where each decision has ramifications, positive or negative.**

Looking back, my memories are little snippets of life, words, and actions that had long-lasting effects. Things that Coach Murphy and Coach Lyons said to me stick with me today—they lit the fires that fueled me through the toughest moments of my career and life. My father probably didn't think much about it at the time, but when he unhesitatingly dove into the water to get the anchor, he changed the course of my future. **Rather than tell me what to do, he did something better that many fail to do: he led by example.** It may not have been a big deal for him, but it was monumental for me. **Not every action requires a discussion.**

Those little moments can shape you for life, teaching you integrity, respect, selflessness, and responsibility. Always strive to be that example—to be the one whose words and actions will influence those around you in a positive and meaningful way. **You never know who is watching.**

FINDING SELF

Becoming a man can mean many things to many people, and most probably have a difficult time narrowing the nebulous process down to a single event. Not me. I can tell you the exact place and time when I crossed the threshold from boy to man. It was a hot and humid summer day in one of the toughest places on the planet: Marine Corps Recruit Depot, Parris Island, South Carolina. Parris Island is an eight-thousand-acre complex located in coastal South Carolina, near the scenic Lowcountry town of Beaufort. Each year, nearly seventeen thousand recruits arrive at the Depot for thirteen grueling weeks of Basic Training, better known as boot camp. Those who emerge do so as United States Marines, a status that I was determined to earn.

Boot camp consists of hour-after-hour, day-after-day of mundane military tasks and harassment from the drill instructors (DIs) for any error, no matter how small. This training in paying close attention to detail is designed to keep Marines alive under fire. We spent countless hours doing rifle drills and marching until those basic military skills were hard-wired into our brains. In order to avoid punishment, everything had to be done in unison with everyone else in the formation, whether it was marching, turning, or manipulating our weapons.

One of the DIs' favorite ways to induce stress and discipline was to require the recruits to stand at rigid attention without moving a muscle, sometimes baking for hours in the brutal sun. Getting caught moving, even the slightest bit, inevitably led to a beat-down session in the infamous Parris Island sand pits. The sand pits, which look just like they sound, are conveniently located everywhere that recruits train so that the DIs constantly have a nearby playground on which to enforce their discipline. For those of you who do not know about Parris Island and its mythical sand fleas, let me tell you, they are very real and extremely annoying and, yes, they love the sand pits.

On this particular day, we were on the drill field practicing, and the sand fleas were biting as normal. I developed, or so I thought, a foolproof plan to tactfully remove the infuriating insects from my body without letting the drill instructors know. We were at "right shoulder arms" with our M-16 rifles rested against the shoulder when I saw a flea land on my bare forearm. I caught myself pleading with it not to bite me, praying that it would move on to one of the other recruits around me. I winced silently as I felt his bite pierce through my skin—the pain was maddening. Using my peripheral vision, I tried to spot each of the ever-vigilant drill instructors so I could remove the painful insect from my arm. When the coast was finally clear, I went for it. As soon as my arm wiped away the bloodsucking insect, I heard the word that every Marine recruit dreads: my own name.

"Recruit Penney, come with me," the closest DI uttered in his deep robotic voice. I quickly broke ranks, knowing what was about to happen, and followed DI Martinez to the nearest sand pit, where the beat-down would commence. Once we got to the pit, I stripped off my gear, as well as the camouflage uniform blouse that I was wearing, and set all of it on the side of the pit with my rifle. Clad in pants, boots, and a T-shirt, I stood facing the instructor, waiting in horror to find out what was in store for me. I had endured these sessions before, but never a one-on-one with a drill instructor, all alone but for us and the fleas. We started with the usual modes of punishment: push-ups, sit-ups, sprints, jumping jacks, and other physical exercises. I was in good physical shape and, though the exercises were tough, they were mainly just annoying. But as the physical effort continued without a break, I moved beyond my physical comfort zone. I could feel the sweat dripping down from my forehead into my eyes, the salty liquid burning—it felt like someone was pouring battery acid onto my face. As time went on I began to fatigue, and I grew more irritated at the situation, wondering if it would ever end. I'm not sure how long I was in that sand pit, but you know you have been somewhere for a long time when the shadows from the trees and other objects are on the complete opposite side from when you arrived.

As the session continued, the DI instructed me, by screaming of course, to run a given distance and back in a certain time.

After the first iteration of this, I realized that the time limits were impossible to meet, and my failure to comply would inevitably lead to another round. It was a no-win situation, and all I could do was my best and hope that he got bored before I collapsed. My irritation level escalated quickly. I can remember visualizing putting my fist through his face, which would have been a great plan, had I been able to lift my arms. The DI would have had his way with me if things got physical; he was a short and stocky Marine with massive arms bursting from under his rolled-up sleeves.

No, fighting wasn't going to help my situation. I had no choice but to submit to his unrelenting physical and psychological punishment. I started to fall into what I call the "feel-sorry-for-me phase," which is never a good place to be. This was another course in mental toughness, one that I only came to appreciate later. As was often the case in my life, I was caught up in the stress of the event, blind to the big picture.

The physical punishment was driving me toward a wall of exhaustion, and I didn't think that I could not take any more of it. After one of the sprints, I stood in the center of the sand pit at the position of attention and started crying. Here I was, a stud high school athlete, dressed in the USMC uniform that I'd long dreamed of wearing, crying like a baby in front of the DI. It was, without a doubt, a defining moment in my life and military career. I stood there, feeling the sweat and tears drip down my face and onto my sodden olive green T-shirt. I was desperately hoping that the drill instructor did not notice that I was crying, but I'm sure that he did; those guys didn't miss anything. I was exactly where he wanted me to be. **I was near my breaking point, and he knew it**. He made me do another sprint, and then another. When I returned, out of breath, I was back in the position of attention in the center of the sand box, still crying and telling myself to pull it together.

Then, something surprising happened. The DI stopped yelling and began to speak to me about discipline, the importance of it, and what poor discipline can lead too: namely, men dying. Swatting a flea on the parade ground seemed harmless, but the same act during an ambush could get someone killed. **While he was speaking, something shifted inside me**.

It was like a button had been pushed, and I instantly knew that I could take any punishment that he was prepared to deliver. Exhausted and defeated only moments earlier, I suddenly felt that this could continue all day and I would not care in the least. He made me do another sprint, but this time I was angry, I wasn't going to feel sorry for myself, and I sure as hell was not going to quit. After a few more iterations, the DI called me over and, as I stood at the familiar position of attention, he looked at me straight in the eyes. He didn't say a word; he just looked at me as if he were reading my thoughts. He knew what had just happened inside me, and I could tell that he was pleased with his results. He had done his job and made me both a man and a Marine.

The starting point. My Marine Corps graduation photo.

From that day forward I knew that, no matter what, I would never quit and I would always keep going, regardless of the circumstances. In the moment, I had no idea how well that never-quit attitude would prove its worth throughout my military career and personal life. I became *unafraid*. That turning point in my mindset no doubt saved my life in later years.

HOT WASH

That day in the sand pits taught me that we humans are amazing creatures. It was the day that I truly got to know myself. My body didn't suddenly become physically stronger or able to endure pain; I simply changed my perspective. Oftentimes, the only thing that we can control in a given situation is our attitude, our mindset. The mind can push the body to do incredible things.

During the opening credits of the movie Lone Survivor, there is a montage of scenes from an actual Basic Underwater Demolition/ SEAL Training (BUD/S) class. The video clips and still images capture recruits who are exhausted, soaking wet, shaking visibly from the cold, and covered in abrasive sand. The instructors are torturing them in the surf zone, ordering the class to do more push-ups than any of them can possibly muster. Their muscles have reached the point of failure, and they lack the strength to do even one more rep.

The quitters quit when their bodies give out, but for the others, it is mind over matter. They fight for every rep as if their very life depends on it, refusing to fail. As the instructor in the scene puts it, "Find an excuse to win!" **The difference between success and failure is often simple mindset, something that can be applied to any aspect of life.**

THE MISS THAT CHANGED MY LIFE

Marine Corps boot camp has two underlying objectives: first to break you down, and then to build you back up. For me, the breaking-down part came to a climax that day in the sand pits; everything from that day forward was easier. (Everything minus going to the bathroom with no door on the stall—not cool and oh, so awkward.)

I've been asked whether I made any friends at Parris Island. The answer is that there's really no time for socializing. I knew the guy to my left and the one to my right, and that's about it. It's a constant grind from the moment the recruit wakes up until he shuts his eyes that night.

We were fed three square meals a day, but there were no snacks, and we were constantly on the move. The result was that we all grew leaner, even those of us with little fat to lose.

We learned all of the basic skills that every Marine should know. Among these was basic rifle marksmanship, the bedrock of the Corps. They say that every Marine is a rifleman, regardless of his or her job title. Unlike the other services, Marine Corps recruits spend a great deal of time on the range during boot camp. Marines are assigned to one of three categories, based on their Qualification Day score: Marksman, Sharpshooter, or Expert. I had dreams of joining the ranks of the legendary Marine Scout Snipers, but achieving that required qualifying as an Expert on the marksmanship test. That was easier said than done, at least for me, anyway.

I believe that the test has changed a bit since I was in boot camp, but in those days it consisted of shooting paper targets at two hundred, three hundred, and five hundred yards. Everything was done with iron sights, which is to say, without the scopes or red dot optics common in today's military. It would be tough enough to see a target at five hundred yards, much less hit it. It was extremely challenging.

I'd had a BB gun as a kid, but I'd never fired a real rifle; I'm not one of those boys who grew up deer hunting or going to the range with their dad. Whether it was my general lack of experience or the fact that I was getting used to my newly issued eyeglasses, I did not excel on the range: I qualified at the lowest level, Marksman, which meant that the dream of attending sniper school would have to wait.

Still, I knew I wanted to be part of something elite and exclusive. One of our drill instructors had served in Force Recon, the Marine's organic special operations force. He wore the scuba bubble badge above the golden jump wings on the breast of his uniform, a sure sign of a Recon Marine. He was a stud, a mentor who touched my life and inspired me without even knowing it. He was fearless when demonstrating rappelling and, as a young and impressionable kid, I wanted to be just like him. First I had to graduate.

My eighteenth birthday fell at some point during boot camp. One of the things recruits learn quickly is to never do anything that draws attention to oneself because the result will not be pretty. I feared a sand-pit-like beatdown from the DIs if they found out it was my birthday, so I kept it a secret. I spent the entire day in fear that someone would find me out and was relieved when I made it to my rack that evening. I can remember lying there, amused that I was spending my eighteenth birthday in such a place. Never, in all of my childhood, had I envisioned "celebrating" my birthday in a place like Parris Island. **The lesson was clear: you never know what life has in store for you**.

After the toughest three months I'd ever experienced, graduation was upon us. I was proud as I marched across the parade ground in my crisp uniform, just as I'd seen the Marines do when I visited my friend's Parris Island graduation the year before. I was a part of something, now: I was a Marine. Both of my parents made the trip to South Carolina, and I know they were immensely proud. I received a few days' leave and went back to Ohio, wearing my red Marine sweatpants while jogging around the neighborhood where I grew up. I was definitely a geek about it.

My next stop was the School of Infantry at Camp Geiger, North Carolina. Camp Geiger is, to put it politely, an armpit. We slept outside for the duration of the school and it was bitterly cold. In those days, the Marines were lowest on the totem pole when it came to military funding and equipment, and we were issued old, outdated gear. Our down-filled sleeping bags were warm, but they weighed a ton when they got wet. It was pretty miserable.

I learned land navigation as well as the basic tactics of a Marine Infantryman, but what I remember most from those months were my efforts to stay warm. I learned tricks, such as lighting a Sterno can in the tent for heat, and discovered that a port-a-potty is surprisingly toasty (you get used to the smell when you are freezing). I would feign having to use the bathroom in order to spend as long as possible there. I remember men being lined up, waiting for me, when I finally opened the door, rubbing my abdomen as if I was having some real problems.

At the end of this training we were given our duty assignments. Even though we weren't at war, I wanted to be in a deployable unit—to be one of the Marines who would take the fight to our enemies when the inevitable call came. In typical military fashion, our desires were ignored "for the good of the Corps." It was decided somewhere that all of the Marines with last names beginning with "P" would head to Quantico, Virginia. When my name was called, I was confused. Quantico was where Security Forces trained, and that wasn't my career path. I raised my hand and asked the instructor why I was headed to Quantico. "To train officers," I was told. What? I didn't know anything, and I was going to be responsible for training the men who would lead other Marines?

Right then and there I decided that, unless I made it to sniper school, I would do my four years in the Marines and then get out. I was there to fight, not to train newly minted second lieutenants. My plan at that point was to go back to Cincinnati and become a cop. I was given three days of leave upon graduation from the School of Infantry, which fell over the Thanksgiving holiday.

I may have been a Marine, but I was still a scared kid who had never traveled by myself, especially on one of the most hectic travel days of the year. The whole thing was poorly organized. I took a Greyhound bus to DC and had to make my way to the airport for a flight to Ohio. I remember walking the streets of the capital, carrying my sea bag, bewildered by the crowd. It took me two days to get to Ohio, and by the time that I made it home, it was pretty much time to head to Quantico.

Marine officers attend Officer Candidates School (OCS) at Quantico before heading to the other side of the base to attend The Basic School (TBS). Every Marine officer, whether they are headed to the Infantry, flight school, or even a clerical job, attends the six-month school. This extended exposure to infantry tactics is one of the things that sets Marine officers apart from their peers in the other services. Having seen it, I believe that every military service should follow the Marine Corps' lead on this.

As it turned out, "training" the new officers actually meant playing war games with them, at least at first. We were to serve as the opposing force for the officers while they learned the basics of infantry life.

It was work, but there were some fun times. My favorite was when we were tasked with infiltrating the officers' patrol bases at night. They were to form a perimeter and the sleep-deprived trainees were to take turns providing security, or at least try to. Our job was to sneak in and "kill" one or more of the officers in the darkness. We got very good at it; it's amazing how brave you can be when no one has live rounds.

We would harass them by placing trip wires and explosive simulators within their lines, keeping them constantly on edge. If we were able to crawl up and make physical contact with an officer, we would whisper to him, "Hand over your bar." (Marine second lieutenants wear a gold bar for rank, and if we got close enough, they would have to hand over their bar as a tangible sign that we had bested them.) It was a bit like counting coup, the Plains Indians' practice of touching their enemies in battle. They considered it a greater honor to touch them harmlessly than to kill them and, since we weren't there to hurt the candidates, we had the same attitude. We instructors wore these captured bars as trophies on the backs of our caps as badges of honor, the same way that college football players earn Ohio State Buckeye or Florida State Tomahawk stickers on their helmets for a job well done. Every once in a while, you would get a first lieutenant or, the Holy Grail, a captain.

My job as an instructor initially put me in the field more than three hundred days per year. This time spent in the Virginia wilderness helped me build a solid foundation of skills that would come in handy later in my career. During this time I also found the niche that would be my comfort zone for the next two decades: Close Quarters Battle (CQB). At Quantico we called it Military Operations in Urban Terrain (MOUT), but by any name it means moving tactically through an urban environment, clearing rooms, and engaging the enemy at close range. CQB can be complicated for some, but all of it just made sense to me, and I took to it almost immediately. I eventually became an instructor, teaching officers the finer points of moving their Marines through complicated scenarios. Though the tactics were slightly different, my time spent doing CQB would pay off in spades when I became a SEAL.

▨　▨　▨

I hadn't really dated in high school, having been so focused on athletics and preparing for the military. It was the same during my early days in the Corps, especially since I was spending so much time in the field.

That changed when I met Leia. She had come down from Annapolis, Maryland, to visit another Marine, but we sort of hit it off. She was dating someone else at the time, but we stayed in touch and were soon spending more and more time together. Without traffic, Annapolis was only about an hour from Quantico, and so we were able to see each other fairly often, despite my work schedule.

Not too long after we began dating, she left me for another Marine. I was crushed. At nineteen, it had been my first real relationship, and now I had experienced my first heartbreak. Within a few weeks she came back, saying that it had all been a big mistake, and we were together from that moment forward.

In hindsight there were plenty of red flags, but I was young and naïve and ignored them. She liked to yell when we would argue, which is a bad trait that I soon adopted. It could be pretty toxic. The biggest warning came one weekend when I was visiting her in Annapolis. I was sitting in the back seat of a car, with Leia and her ex-boyfriend sitting up front, an uncomfortable enough situation on its own. Things got really weird, though, when the two of them started doing hard drugs right in front of me. I had never so much as seen narcotics before then and, as far as I was concerned, just being in the car put my career in jeopardy. I guess young love endures all.

We married in a small church ceremony in Annapolis, and the reception was held afterward at her parents' house. Here we were, me a nineteen-year-old Marine and she a twenty-one-year-old waitress, beginning our lives as a married couple.

She moved down to Virginia and we began to build a life together. I was still spending most of my days and some of my nights out training. Broke Marines didn't have cell phones in those days, so we had minimal contact during the week.

I came home one Friday night and there was a gift waiting for me; it was an Abercrombie & Fitch sweater, the height of 1990s fashion. With it was a note in my wife's handwriting, breaking the news that I was going to be a father. I wasn't even old enough to drink and could barely take care of myself, and now I was going to be responsible for another human life? I was terrified, but at the same time excited.

■   ■   ■

The Marine Corps is very structured, and the chain of command is everything. As an individual rifleman, your fire team leader is your boss, your mentor, and your only real outlet when it comes to problem solving. Feeling sick? Talk to your team leader. Having financial problems? Talk to your team leader. Need to know how a weapons system works? Talk to your team leader.

Because of the power this position holds over the lives of individual Marines, team leaders can make your life pleasant or downright miserable. Fortunately for me, my team leader was a stud. Sergeant Fox wasn't a big guy physically, but he was imposing nonetheless. He kept his dirty blond hair buzzed tight, and looked at you with piercing blue eyes. I'm not sure where he was born, but he spoke with an English accent. He had come from a deployable unit at Camp Pendleton, which meant that he knew what it was like to be a real Marine. He had all of the attributes of an endurance athlete and could run or ruck march all day without ever seeming to tire. **He had one other quality, one that gave him God-like status: he was a sniper.**

Fox was a master of fieldcraft, and his gear was always squared away. If he lost his pack on an operation, he had all of the right gear on his belt to survive without it. Everything was thought out, organized, and right where it needed to be. He seemed to know everything when it came to soldiering, and I wanted to be just like him.

At roughly two years into my career, Fox organized a training trip for our fire team. Our objective was to learn mountaineering skills so that we could teach the officers. It was fall when we drove in a pair of white vans to the mountains of West Virginia for our three-day school.

This may seem like a little thing but, for the first time since I'd been at Quantico, this trip was not about the officers, it was about us. We learned everything from knot tying to using pulley systems to lift heavy objects. We were trained in the use of various harnesses, carabiners, and figure-eight descenders. We made rope bridges and rappelled down mountains. I ate it up.

This trip opened my eyes to the reality that there was more out there than doing grunt work and following orders. This little taste of individual training left me hungry for more—I wanted to learn everything, go to every school, and master every skill. I knew that being assigned to some type of special unit was the key to achieving this goal. In those days, there were only two options: force recon and sniper. Scout snipers are legendary in the Marine Corps, but Sergeant Fox made that career path even more attractive. I set my sights on earning a slot into sniper school.

Back at my job, I'd watch as Marines who had received orders to Quantico's Marine Corps Scout Sniper School readied their gear for the training ahead. They would spend their spare time painstakingly constructing their 3-D camouflage ghillie suits by hand. I could not have been more envious. Marines usually qualify with their weapon once a year but, since I was determined to make Expert and qualify for the sniper program, I was allowed repeated attempts. I begged Sergeant Fox to qualify as often as possible, and he did his best to work up the chain of command and make it happen. I became increasingly proficient and progressed to the Sharpshooter level, always falling just short of the score that I needed. Marines have to have so many years left on their contract to attend sniper school, and I was informed that I would be given one last chance to qualify before I hit that deadline.

I did my best, but on my final attempt, I missed Expert by a single round. It would be a miss that would change the course of my life, and I know now that it wasn't meant to be. My destiny was elsewhere and, had I made that shot, I probably would have never left the Marine Corps. As it was, I was crushed—my dreams of serving in an elite combat unit were shattered, and there was no question that I would get out once I'd served my four years. I'd begun working on my criminal justice degree, and I considered a career in the FBI. Soon after, my daughter, Kailha, was born, and it was time to focus on providing a good, stable life for my family.

Kailha was a beautiful baby, with an olive complexion, dark brown hair, and enormous brown eyes. She may have looked more like her mother but, from the start, she was Daddy's girl. I would hold her for hours, just looking at her precious little face. I never knew that I could love someone as much as I loved her. Like most men, becoming a father changed my life for the better.

There is no instruction manual for being a dad and, at only nineteen years old, I was pretty unprepared. I deferred to my wife on most of the day-to-day tasks of parenting, especially since I was still spending a lot of time in the field training. I tried to help as best I could and, if I was home, I would take over the late-night feedings. There isn't much that is more peaceful than bottle-feeding a baby in the middle of the night. The house is dark and dead silent, but for the humming of the air conditioner and the funny little noises that babies make. It gave me lots of time for reflection, particularly about my career. Was it selfish of me to pursue my own dreams when I now had this little person's welfare to think about?

Was I really now destined to become a federal agent, or a Cincinnati cop? The desire that had been with me since childhood still remained: the more I thought about it, the more I began to consider transitioning to the Navy in order to give the SEAL dream a go.

I did my research and spoke to Navy recruiters, preparing for life's next challenge with my wife's support. I found out that there was no way to make an immediate jump; I would have to serve my entire Marine contract and separate from the service for a day before I could become a sailor. I would also lose two of my hard-earned stripes, but I didn't care; all I wanted to do was become a frogman.

I loved a great deal about the Marine Corps, but there were aspects of the culture that just didn't work for me. One such thing that helped me make my decision to leave was the Corps' obsession with rank. I was at work one day, sweeping the floor of a GP medium tent while I was being "supervised" by another Marine. He was a corporal and I was a lance corporal, merely one rank below him—he probably made $50 more per month than I did. I was at the corner of the tent, pulling on the broom in an attempt to sweep some dirt away from the wall, when he stopped me.

"What kind of broom is that?" the corporal asked in a harsh tone.

"It's a push broom," I responded.

"Then push it, don't pull it," he said, with disgust in his voice. Here I was, doing my job, and he was treating me like an idiot just because he could. He struck me as the kind of kid who got beat up in high school and now hid behind his rank. I dropped the broom right in front of him and walked away from the tent without another word. I was done.

HOT WASH

I failed, I failed, and I failed again. Failure is a part of life, and it will only make you stronger. I was devastated when I realized that I would never be a Marine sniper, and I thought my military career was over. Sometimes, though, you fail for a reason; our paths in life aren't always linear. If I'd made that shot, I would have never fulfilled my dream of becoming a SEAL. I didn't allow my failure to define me; instead I picked myself up and drove forward until I was at the very tip of the spear. You will fail—in school, at work, or in your relationships. Don't quit, and never stop pushing forward. There is a plan for our lives, but we don't get briefed on it—figuring it out is part of the adventure.

MANDATORY BUD/S CHAPTER

BUD/S stands for Basic Underwater Demolition/SEAL training. This six-month course and its sadistic instructors are the gatekeepers to the SEAL community. Cold water and chafing sand are their legendary torture implements.

Every BUD/S class has a number, and that class number follows you for the rest of your life, much in the way one's graduating class from high school does. More than one fake SEAL has been exposed when he couldn't give his class number. I would be part of Class 237. I packed up the family and drove west, renting an apartment in Chula Vista, California, so that I could spend as much time as possible with my wife and daughter as I trained.

At last, I had made it to the famed Southern California beaches where sailors were transformed into SEALs. I had waited much of my life for this moment, but there was a bit more waiting yet to endure. Nothing happens fast in the conventional military; it took nearly a year from the time that I entered the Navy until I stepped foot on the famed beaches of the Silver Strand. The details aren't important, but much of this time involved learning how to fold clothes correctly. Seriously.

First I had to go through BUD/S Indoctrination, or Indoc, which was five weeks long. On my first day at Coronado, I checked in at the BUD/S compound, wearing my dress uniform. Even though I was new to the Navy I had a couple of ribbons on my chest, thanks to my time in the Marines. The Navy uses a ribbon instead of a metal badge to designate marksmanship ability, so I had traded my Marine Sharpshooter badge for a Navy Sharpshooter ribbon. One of the BUD/S instructors walked up to me and looked at my uniform. "Sharpshooter, huh?" he said as he tapped the ribbon on my dress whites. "We're going to make that an Expert." That was my first glimpse into the SEAL culture and mindset: people matter, and we are here to make you better. His words inspired me. Looking back, it is amazing to think how just a few simple words could have lasting results, just as they'd had on me as a kid. **Point taken: be that force that touches the lives of others.**

In hindsight, it was probably pretty bold to think that I could become a SEAL after never so much as qualifying for sniper school in the Marine Corps. I didn't think of it in those terms, though; I just knew what I wanted to do. I felt a passion that I'd never experienced before, and, for the first time in my life, I knew the real meaning of that word. If I didn't try, I would spend the rest of my life wondering what could have been. For some reason there was no doubt in my mind that I would make it—I just knew that it was meant to be. I would have to do my part, though. Before leaving the Marines I'd started running, lifting hard, and even swimming in my cammies to get into shape. I'd worked harder than I'd ever worked before, doing everything that I could to mentally and physically prepare myself for the ultimate challenge.

The BUD/S compound is surprisingly small, especially when compared to the schools I'd seen in the Marine Corps. It mainly consists of 1960s-era two-story concrete buildings that house the classrooms and offices. It honestly looks more like a junior high school than it does the training ground for some of America's most elite warriors.

The buildings form a courtyard known as the "grinder," which is where much of our future punishment and improvement would take place. Instead of the painted boot prints I'd seen at Parris Island, each trainee's position on the grinder is marked with a pair of stenciled swim fins. A life-size Creature from the Black Lagoon statue wearing a web belt and a dive knife stands ominously to the side, holding a sign that reads, "So you want to be a frogman."

During Indoc, around ninety of us prospective SEALs checked in daily at 6 a.m. and essentially did physical training (PT) until noon. We ran, we swam, and we had our first experience with the unforgiving sand and frigid water that would help the instructors torture our bodies over the next six months. It was good preparation for something that no one can be 100 percent prepared for. I was in good physical shape but it really didn't matter: no matter how fit you were, they were going to break you down into cookie dough when BUD/S began. It didn't matter if you could do one hundred push-ups or one thousand, the instructors would push you to the limit and beyond, and you wouldn't be able to do a single rep when they were done with you. They gave a new meaning to muscle failure.

At Indoc, I felt my priorities shift from my family to my career. It was inevitable. I justified it by the thought that making the Teams would help the family financially. SEALs receive dive pay, demo pay, jump pay, plus other incentives. Becoming a SEAL would have a significant effect on our small family's monthly budget.

The extra money was nice, but it was really all about me. I gave the family my weekends, but during the week, the training was everything.

I finally felt at home. As soon as you arrive in Coronado, your identification as a SEAL begins. Your fellow trainees and instructors look at you as a potential future teammate—someone on whom their life might one day depend. It was a men's club where high standards of physical fitness, dress, and attention to detail were the norm. The term "alpha male" is taboo these days, but that's what we were, ninety or so alpha males, sizing one another up like lions preparing to fight. It was a bit like being a star on your high school football team and then showing up at a Division One college—it raised the bar for all of us.

Hardly an old man at twenty-four, I was still one of the oldest members of Class 237. I believe that my age was an advantage. There was a huge difference between the seventeen-year-old kid who had stepped off the bus in Parris Island, and who I was at twenty-four at BUD/S. My time in the Marine Corps, not to mention the realities of fatherhood, had matured me, as well as hardened my mind and body.

When you are about to embark on one of the toughest training courses in the world, there are a lot of naysayers who can put doubts into your head. "The dropout rate is 75 percent, you know," they would say. "Hell Week is tough; everyone quits." Despite their warnings, I knew that quitting was not in my future. Thanks to my punishment at the hands of Drill Instructor Martinez that day in the Parris Island sand pits, I knew that I could do it. Barring a serious injury, I was going to be a SEAL.

The strangest part of Indoc for me was the mindset of some of my future classmates. They seemed genuinely surprised that the water here was actually cold, as if they'd done no research whatsoever. Other candidates spoke of "practicing" for sleep deprivation. Huh? You can't prepare for that—all you will do is get more tired.

I'm often asked whether I regret the time I spent in the Marine Corps before I transitioned to the Navy. The answer is a firm "no." Not only did it make me more mature, but there were practical advantages, as well. Four years of spending countless nights in the field had taught me that I could endure physical discomfort and, unlike the sailors coming from training or the fleet, I had a solid base of infantry skills from which to draw upon. That maturity and experience would serve me well once training began.

There was a final piece in the puzzle too: I'd seen enough of the conventional Navy to know how bad life would suck if I didn't make it through BUD/S. I had no desire to spend the next four years plodding through life as a gunner's mate on a ship. Failure was not an option.

BUD/S is divided into three phases of two months each. First Phase is a physical beat-down, designed to weed out the weak before the real training begins. The famed "Hell Week" takes place during First Phase, around week five. Second Phase is the diving portion of the course, where trainees learn to be comfortable underwater and with using scuba equipment and other diving techniques. Third Phase is the land warfare phase, when weapons, tactics, and explosives are taught and then put into action. Due to injuries and illness, it is very common for BUD/S candidates to be rolled back to the beginning of a phase with a later class in order to complete their training. Because of these roll-ins, our group of 90 swelled to 150 when it was finally time to class up. Six years after I'd swiped the issue of *Popular Mechanics* with the cover shot of the SEAL wading out of the Coronado surf, it was finally my chance to prove that I had what it took. Class 237 was about to begin.

■ ■ ■

It was late summer of 2001 when we began: day one, week one. I couldn't wait for it to start. Once it started, I couldn't wait for it to end.

There is no single part of BUD/S that makes it so brutal; it is the cumulative result of the thousands of physical and mental challenges the trainees are subjected to on a daily basis. It's a grind that seems like it will never end. The only way to swallow it is one bite at a time. Just get me through this run, through this exercise, through this swim. If I can make it to lunch, I'll be fine. And so it went, hour by hour, day by day, month by month.

There is a very specific uniform for BUD/S candidates, one that makes it instantly clear what stage of the training an individual is in. Most of the time you wear pants and a 1980s-style, long-sleeve, woodland-pattern-camouflage blouse with a T-shirt under it.

The cammies become saturated with water quickly and dry very slowly, adding the additional weight of a soaking wet uniform to every task. You wear a web belt that holds a canteen along with a short length of line. If there is nothing else going on, you'd better have that line out, practicing your knot-tying.

At the start of training, that T-shirt is white. The white T-shirt means that you haven't yet made it through Hell Week. Only when and if you've passed that hurdle do you trade your white T-shirt in for a brown one.

The World War II-era UDT (Underwater Demolition Team) shorts are another distinctive piece of SEAL gear. These Magnum, P.I.-length nut huggers leave very little to the imagination (they reminded me of my Speedo days as a swimmer). Besides being so revealing, the UDT shorts chafe horribly.

Then there's the helmet. Each BUD/S candidate wears a fiberglass helmet that is painted a specific color for each phase of training. During First Phase you wear a green helmet, in Second Phase it is blue, and in Third Phase it is painted red. Your last name, class, and rank are stenciled onto the helmet, and each candidate is responsible for ensuring that the helmet stays painted perfectly throughout the six-month course. Carefully repainting the helmet is how a candidate spends most weekends, particularly after an instructor slams that helmet down on the asphalt grinder, shattering the paint job.

First Phase was all about thinning the herd, and the quitting began almost immediately. When a candidate quits, he has to ring the brass ship's bell that hangs in a corner of the grinder. During Hell Week, the ever-thoughtful instructors bring the bell right out onto the beach to make quitting that much easier. All you have to do to make the pain, the cold, and the exhaustion stop is to ring the bell. After a candidate quits, his helmet is placed on the ground beside the bell as a tangible symbol of the unreal attrition rate. There was no way that my helmet was going to join the growing row; no chance that I was going to ring that bell. The more helmets I saw lined up on the grinder, the more motivated I became. It was a boost of energy every time.

If you've ever seen a movie or a television show about the SEALs, you've probably seen images of what BUD/S life is like. For those that haven't, it's pretty simple: trainees are subjected to hours upon hours of running in soft sand, thousands of repetitions of calisthenics, negotiating a challenging obstacle course, and the constant harassment of the instructors. Added to this is the constant chafing of skin thanks to the sand- and salt-crusted cammies and near-constant exposure to the frigid waters of the Pacific Ocean.

The cold water is what gets most of the quitters. There doesn't seem to be any outwardly visible rhyme or reason to why some quit, while others refuse. Some of the most impressive athletes in my class quit quickly, and some guys that I didn't think had a chance made it all the way through.

There were some surprises. I was naturally drawn toward the guys who could display humor during the most punishing moments of the training, and there was one trainee who will go down as one of the funniest people I've ever been around. The instructors would march us out into the surf to be pounded by the freezing waves, hour after hour. Every time a wave was about to hit us he would scream, "Oh, no! Look out!" at the top of his lungs. The first time was funny, but the two-hundredth time was downright hilarious. I assumed that he would breeze through BUD/S, lifting all of us up along the way; I was shocked when, on the third day, he simply quit.

BUD/S is all about teamwork; nothing is about the individual other than his effort to make the team function. Each candidate has a "swim buddy," who is essentially your partner in everything you do. Three to four pairs of swim buddies make up a boat crew, and your six- to eight-man boat crew is essentially your team. When trainees quit, instructors will consolidate boat crews to keep the numbers reasonably even. There were some solid men on my crew, some of whom went on to great things later in life. I was surrounded by truly impressive people.

Our days usually started with a long run on the beach or a swim in the ocean, followed by a beat-down on the grinder. Classes were mixed in among the physical events, and we began to learn the basic skills that all frogmen must possess. Running was never my thing, and I was often on the "goon squad," which is the cohort of the slowest runners. I would have rather done squats and push-ups until my muscles completely failed than do the runs. Still, they were part of the program, so I pushed myself to do my best. Thanks to my background as a swimmer, water was my comfort zone, and my swim buddy and I were always among the fastest on the ocean swims.

We complemented each other's strengths and weaknesses: he was a strong runner, and I was a strong swimmer. I would pace off him during runs, and he would do the same in the water. One day we were doing a two-mile ocean swim, side-stroking our way to the instructor in his kayak and back. Out of nowhere, I spotted a giant marine animal swimming directly toward me. My brain was screaming "shark!" though it turned out to be a sea lion. He swerved right before he would have run into me and disappeared into the murky water. I seriously think that my swim buddy and I both came completely out of the water trying to escape becoming something's lunch. It scared the heck out of us and, with our adrenaline surging from the fright, we finished that swim in what must have been record time.

The instructors all had their particular physical strengths and would exploit them to challenge us. Some instructors were strong runners, preferring to punish the class on the grinder, while others pushed us in the water. One instructor was an especially strong runner, and I always dreaded the runs that he led. You could tell how bad it was going to be by the shoes he was wearing: he had painted flames on the sides of his black government-issued Bates boots, and if he showed up wearing those, we knew we were in for a rough one.

As bad as BUD/S sucked, I actually had fun—not the kind of fun you get when you ride a roller coaster and feel good in the moment, but the kind of fun that you realize only later, and truly appreciate when you look back on it.

One thing that I really liked about BUD/S was the fact that we, the candidates, were the focus of the training. When I was in the Marine Corps, our focus had been on training the officers; everything was about them. In BUD/S, it was all about us. I soaked up every class and relished learning every new skill, however mundane and seemingly trivial.

I still had a family, though, and, other than when we had a night swim or something that ran particularly late, I would go home to our apartment at night. If I was lucky, Kailha would still be awake, and I would get a chance to see her before bedtime.

The weekends were all about letting my body recover from the abuse of the week, and I spent many a Saturday lying on the couch. My little girl would bring her blanket and climb up on top of my chest so that we could watch TV together. I can see her now, dragging that tattered hunk of cloth and sucking on two of her fingers instead of a pacifier. She was my little version of Linus from the *Peanuts* cartoons. Thinking back, those were some of the happiest moments of my life.

Though I lived off-base, I still had a room on the compound and was responsible for keeping it in perfect condition. The instructors would inspect our rooms and punish us severely for the smallest infraction. Inspection was basically impossible to pass. You might spend half of your Sunday preparing your room for an inspection, only to have it ransacked by the instructors for a single grain of sand found on the floor. On weekends, when I wasn't cleaning my room or snuggling with my daughter, I was touching up the paint job on my helmet, preparing for another week.

The climax of First Phase is Hell Week, which takes place in the fifth week of training. It begins on Sunday afternoon and runs on a defined schedule until Friday afternoon. The only thing that isn't on the schedule is sleep.

Try as you might, you won't be able to sleep on Sunday due to nervous anticipation, which means that the candidates are essentially awake for six days. Not only is there little or no sleep—there is constant physical activity and harassment. The instructors work in shifts, and additional SEALs are brought in for the week to ensure that there are enough cadre members to keep up the punishment for twenty-four hours a day. It's far harder than your mind can comprehend, but if you can endure it, you will learn an awful lot about yourself, both physically and mentally. It is amazing what the human body is capable of, and Hell Week might be the ultimate example of mind over matter.

A number of my fellow trainees were nervous about Hell Week. Candidly, I was not. My attitude going in was "I'm finally here." Sure, I knew I would be tired, and I knew it would be cold, and I knew it was going to suck, but I had the right attitude about it. This was what I had read about in the magazines and seen in the movies; this was what I'd signed up for. It's my time. I'm here, I'm ready, let's go.

Everyone knows exactly when Hell Week will start and when it will end, but you're never really certain until it happens. When the sun goes down on Sunday evening, the trainees wait impatiently inside a classroom. BOOM! The jarring sound and flash of an artillery simulator pierces though the night sky, followed by the deafening rattle of belt-fed M60 machine guns, firing blanks. The instructors create instant chaos as the class spills out into the grinder to begin the week.

Two of my friends and I handled the beginning of Hell Week in a pretty entertaining way: we essentially ran around like we were on some mission, all the while avoiding the instructors. We would hide in a classroom until an instructor found us, and then we would rush off to "get a head count" before finding another place to hide. They would tell us to "get wet and sandy," and we would run off like we were going to do it, racing instead to our next hideout. We spent about three hours ducking the instructors before they caught on to what we were doing. These tiny mental victories helped fuel our morale.

During Hell Week, your boat crew must take its inflatable boat everywhere. These boats weigh over two hundred pounds dry, and even more when an instructor decides to shovel in some wet sand. You might go for a three-mile run on the beach, balancing that heavy boat on your head the entire way. Going to eat chow? You're taking the boat. The boats force teamwork both in and out of the water and are one of the instructors' greatest tools during Hell Week. You even have to take the boats through the obstacle course, which absolutely focuses the team, since every member of the crew must pull his weight.

Candidates are lucky if they manage even three hours of sleep during Hell Week, but thanks to the unbelievable number of calories that are burned in a given day, trainees are usually given plenty to eat; we all pretty much lived meal-to-meal. But when the time arrived to have our first meal of Hell Week, our dreams of getting a few quiet moments to sit and eat were shattered. Instead of sitting down at a table, we sat *outside* the chow hall—with our boats on our heads. We were each given an MRE (Meals Ready to Eat), of which we were only allowed to eat the main entrée. If your main meal wasn't good, you ate it anyway and hoped for better next time.

We spent a great deal of time in the water that week. The instructors would tell us to "get wet and sandy," which meant we had to jump into the cold ocean and then roll around in the sand until we had a nice coating of the abrasive in every crevice of our bodies. We would link arms and march into the surf, where waves would crash into us over and over.

The quitting began almost immediately. It always amazed me that men who had waited years for this moment quit as soon as the instructors turned up the heat on us. Many of them were great guys, and I wonder if the regret of quitting nags at them still. I swear that there are blocks on the instructors' Hell Week training schedule that read "09001000 hours: Make someone quit." There is a reason for everything that the instructors do, though; the system works.

By Wednesday, you are pretty much clinically insane due to the lack of sleep. The instructors are looking for the individuals who can push themselves beyond that point and still function. Standing with our heavy inflatable boats on our heads, we would hear a "thud" as a trainee fell asleep on his feet and collapsed. Others passed out at meals, their faces dropping into full trays of food. Delusions and hallucinations were common. I was paddling in the ocean with my boat crew when one of them said he could see the menu for our planned post-Hell Week dinner up in the sky. "I can see it: steak, lobster..." he read down the list as he pointed to the empty air ahead of us. In the moment, it seemed totally reasonable. (For me, things became very distorted—it was almost like I was underwater; I also heard voices.) Such things kept us slap-happy in the moment and kept the mood relatively light.

The nights were worse than the days, at least for me. My low point came on Thursday night, when the instructors herded us to the bay side of the Coronado peninsula and had us all lie in the shallow brackish water, with only our faces sticking out. Our feet were on the beach and the rest of our bodies were in the water.

After being helplessly pounded by cold Pacific waves for days, this innovation had seemed pretty tame at first. Then we felt the biting. Some small marine creatures—whether they were insects or some type of tiny shrimp, I'll never know—were working their way under our soaked clothing and biting our exposed skin. It was like the sand pits in Parris Island, but worse, since we had already been pushed to the limit. The feeling of frustration was overwhelming: my mind deadened by the lack of sleep, my first thought was, "Don't they know that something is biting us?" Had I had any of my wits about me, I would have realized that this was exactly why they had brought us here: to find a new button to push.

My Hell Week experience took what I'd learned about the human mind to an entirely new level. The reason that I am so high on "mindset" is that I have seen what we are capable of with the proper frame of mind. The body is done, but the brain is still pushing. **If you're going to be in a bad situation, having a bad attitude can only make it worse. My mindset was the only part of the training that I could control.** Though Hell Week was certainly punishing and you couldn't pay me enough to do it again, I never gave quitting any serious thought—the instructors would have to kill me if they didn't want me to wear a Trident.

(The Trident is the SEAL emblem, composed of elements of sea, air, and land, from which SEALs derive their acronym. The centerpiece of the badge is Neptune's trident, which symbolizes the sea as well as our roots in underwater demolition. The eagle represents the air, from which we will come if necessary. The pistol is evidence of our commitment to land warfare; it is cocked because we are always ready for the fight. The oversized gold Trident badge on the chest of your uniform lets the world know that you are a Navy SEAL.)

No one in my boat crew quit that week, either. Our team stayed together, and we fed off one another's energy.

When the sun came up on Friday morning, I can remember feeling its warmth on my skin. After shivering like a jackhammer all night, this was wonderful. It raised my spirits, and I knew that when the sun went down again, I would be done.

One of the last things they did was to give us a series of combination locks that were locked together in one giant mass. We were each given a combination and told to release our assigned lock. The combinations were all wrong, of course, but we were too delirious to notice. One of the trainees was overcome by frustration, and he yelled out in panic, "This Hell Week is never going to end!" We all knew that it would be over in a matter of hours, but our minds were so warped by then that it was difficult to tell what was real from what we were imagining.

That afternoon we stood in formation, ready for the next round of abuse. We stood in stunned silence, all of us at the absolute edge of our ability to function at even a basic level. Instead of more yelling and orders, the instructors shouted, "BUD/S Class 237 is secure from Hell Week!" Those were the sweetest words that I'd ever heard. It was over.

Half of the class that we'd started with had rung the bell; dozens of discarded helmets and dreams lined the grinder. We who had made it would trade our white T-shirts for brown ones, a tangible symbol of the change in our minds that would last forever. I felt an immense sense of pride.

HOT WASH

"We will make you into an Expert." That one little comment changed my outlook and put me in a mindset where I could not fail. Every individual has the power to give life, motivation, and a "can do" attitude. That same voice can bring negativity and doubt. Remember that, when speaking to others, words matter.

BUD/S isn't about the cold water, the abrasive sand, the long runs, or the lack of sleep. Those are merely tools that the instructors use to make you find your own personal limits. Those limits are symptoms of the disease of misery. To make it through BUD/S, you need to find a way to break down those barriers. The battle is inside your own mind. Sure, BUD/S was tough. Combat is tough. Life is tough. We can't always count on an easy path; your attitude is what makes the difference between success and failure, between happiness and sorrow. **Refuse to quit on life**.

FIND YOUR BATHTUB

The few days after Hell Week were a blur; I did my best to catch up on sleep before we got back to work on Monday. The next week was Walk Week, where the instructors took it a bit easier on us to let our bodies recover.

The final obstacle of First Phase was Over-The-Beach Week, which was spent learning the ins and outs of hydrographic reconnaissance, a skill that goes back to the origins of the SEAL Teams. UDTs (Underwater Demolition Teams) were the predecessors to the SEALs. These brave men would swim in close to hostile beaches, often at night, carrying minimal gear. Besides removing physical obstacles that would interfere with an amphibious landing, they carefully mapped the sea floor, currents, and tides where the landing would take place. When the US Marines landed on the beaches during the Pacific Campaign during World War II, they were often met by signs erected by the UDTs, "welcoming" them to the island.

Honestly, I found this to be one of the more challenging units in the training. I was still incredibly tired and a bit hydrophobic from Hell Week—the mere thought of cold water was enough to make me shudder. Regardless, we were back in the water constantly, trying to make our brains function on three to four hours' sleep as we worked to chart the ocean floor. It was like a second Hell Week for me—it was especially hard because I wasn't expecting it to be so challenging.

First Phase ended without much drama, and each of us prepared ourselves for the Second Phase: diving. We had made it through the toughest one-third of the training, but the pace didn't decrease at all. That weekend, we painted our helmets blue, and then we were back at it on Monday.

Second Phase is what turns sailors into frogmen as they learn the finer points of diving, using both open- and closed-circuit breathing equipment. Open-circuit is standard scuba gear through which the diver inhales compressed air and exhales carbon dioxide into the water. The problem with this for combat operations is that the enemy can spot the bubbles, revealing that there are divers in the water. The solution is a closed-circuit system that uses soda lime to scrub the carbon dioxide and then recycles the air back into the diver's breathing hose. The result is a complete absence of bubbles, enabling SEALs to move stealthily into harbors and other targets.

SEAL trainees are introduced to these diving techniques in the pool before venturing into open waters through a process that culminates in what's known as pool comp, two or three weeks into Second Phase. Like Hell Week, pool comp is a main attrition event.

Some individuals just can't make themselves sufficiently comfortable in the water, and pool comp weeds them out of the class. There is a list of tasks that each candidate must complete underwater, which includes taking off your gear and putting it back on. The instructors do everything they can to physically disorient the candidate, who is trying to breath underwater using scuba gear. The instructors will spin him around, tie his air hose into knots, and do anything else that can to make him lose his cool.

The thing that got me was when they tied my exhalation knot, preventing me from exhaling. I flipped out. I had to learn to inhale through my mouth and exhale through my nose. It's more difficult than it sounds, and I struggled with it. If I couldn't figure it out, I would fail pool comp, and my dreams would be shattered. The thought of spending months or even years at a time working on a ship while my wife and daughter sat in an apartment was terrifying.

I had to find a way. I didn't have a pool available after hours, so I found the next best thing: my apartment's bathtub. Every night I would come home, play with Kailha, and then grab a snorkel and head for the tub. I spent hours face down in the water, learning how to calmly exhale through my nose. Once I got comfortable with that, I was good.

Not everyone was able to find a solution to their particular hang-up, though. Some really tough guys, who excelled during First Phase, fell victim to these mental hurdles. One of my buddies, who is a complete physical stud and went on to have a successful EOD (Explosive Ordnance Disposal) career, couldn't make it through pool comp. I don't know where I would be today without that bathtub.

Once through pool comp, trainees learn how to use the German-made Draeger closed-circuit breathing apparatus. Using it sounds simple, but it's not—do it wrong and you'll die.

Though Second Phase is more technical, the instructors don't cut us any slack. As soon as they saw the class begin to slip in terms of discipline or attention to detail, they would smoke us. If they wanted you dressed for a dive in thirty seconds, that meant thirty seconds. They would make us dress and undress for hours until we could do it in the allotted time.

We dove day and night, learning to navigate underwater with one swim buddy following a compass mounted to a small plastic board while counting his kicks to judge distance. The other diver's job is to look out for unseen obstacles in the water. Given my comfort level in the water and my background as a competitive swimmer, I felt very much at home, at least during the day.

Daytime dives are fun; there's a reason why people pay good money to go scuba diving. Night diving, on the other hand, is scary. The darkness allows your imagination to run wild; since you can't see what is in the surrounding waters, you simply assume that there are sharks lurking everywhere. No Navy frogman had been killed by a shark since 1963, but that fact gave us little comfort.

During one night dive, my swim buddy and I decided that we would swim as fast as possible, so that we could rest on the boat afterward. We powered through the event and were the first pair to arrive at the buoy that marked the finish line. Little did we know, we would have to wait for the rest of the class to finish before we could get out of the water. We clung to that buoy for what seemed like hours. Each time one of us inadvertently hit the other underwater with one of our swim fins, we would jump with fear: "What was that?"

There were two dives per day that lasted two hours each (any longer than that and the nitrogen levels in the body could become deadly). At least one of these dives would take place at night. We learned how to follow the contours of the ocean and to sneak undetected into an active harbor, where we placed simulated mines on the hulls of Navy ships. This may seem like an antiquated skill, but during the 1989 invasion of Panama, four divers from SEAL Team Two swam undetected and placed explosives on the presidential yacht of Manuel Noriega. The boat was destroyed, eliminating one of the leader's potential means of escape.

I thought I had it tackled since surviving pool comp, but it turned out that one of the toughest parts of BUD/S for me was to be another Second Phase event. It required each of us to tread water, using only our legs, for a full five minutes—AND while wearing twin eighty-cubic-feet capacity metal scuba tanks, which together weighed roughly eighty-five pounds. Our hands were to be raised over our heads and had to stay out of the water the entire time.

I made it on my first try, but it was incredibly difficult. Fifteen seconds in, I was smoked; I'm a big guy, have very little body fat, and don't float very well. The adult human head weighs ten to eleven pounds, so I would dip my head under water to give myself a break. My legs were screaming, my breathing was labored, and, although I was in the water, I was still sweating profusely. The bathtub couldn't help me prepare for this one—I just had to endure. **Push aside the pain and panic. Get it done. Once again, it was all about not quitting.**

After you make it through Hell Week and pool comp, unless you do something stupid, you're probably going to make it. At a certain point, just about anything can become routine, and BUD/S became a sort of job, albeit a tough one. I would get up each morning and drive to the base for work, and then, most nights, I could head home, able to spend as much time as possible with my family. My wife and I got along well, probably because I was so focused on BUD/S.

The lack of drama at home was great, but it wouldn't last. Everyone's world, including mine, was about to be rocked.

It was a fall Tuesday morning, which started off just like any other. I left my apartment early that morning and made the quiet drive to the BUD/S compound in the dark. After a pre-dawn workout, we were in the chow hall getting breakfast. While I was putting my tray down on the table, I saw a group of instructors gathered around a television screen. As the camera zoomed in, we saw the now-iconic images of the burning North Tower of the World Trade Center in New York. Moments later we watched in horror as a passenger- and fuel-laden airliner disappeared into the South Tower in a ball of fire. Men and women, who had gone to work that day to earn a living for their families, jumped to their deaths on live television to avoid the searing heat and smoke.

We knew immediately that it was an act of terrorism and that everything had changed. The United States was no longer at peace. We weren't training just to train—we were training for war. It was all real then, and every day took on new meaning, because we knew we would be called upon to put our skills to the test in the real world, against the men who had planned this attack. Rumors almost immediately began to fly around the class that we were going to graduate early and rush off to the Middle East to begin the fight.

That didn't happen, but nearly everyone in that room would find themselves in the thick of it before long. Little did we know that our nation would be constantly at war for the next two decades. I wanted to fight for my country, and I was going to get my wish.

▪ ▪ ▪

Third Phase of BUD/S is the Land Warfare phase, which is when the firearm and explosive training begins. For me, it was fun, but also a bit dangerous, inasmuch as none of us had been around explosives before.

The instructors were methodical, training us step-by-step to make sure we didn't blow ourselves up. Someone usually messed up anyway, though. One time, the instructors told us to "prepare to pull smoke." A trainee took that as simply "pull smoke," and ignited his charge prematurely. As punishment, the instructors made him carry the M4000, a gigantic fake rifle that weighs a ton. Carrying it lets the entire world know that you've made a colossal error; it's the Third Phase version of a dunce cap.

I'd shot plenty in the Marines, but primarily using the M16 rifle. In Third Phase we got to shoot all of the toys: MP5 submachine guns, handguns, you name it. We learned basic smallunit tactics and became comfortable moving as a team while shooting with live ammunition. I had a blast, and thanks to the solid foundation of skills I'd acquired during my time in the Marine Corps, I stood out. In the Marine Corps, it was all about rank, uniforms, and haircuts. In the Teams, it is all about how well you can do your job. Your teammates care more about whether you can shoot than what rank you wear on your sleeve.

Things really began to click for me. The physical beat-downs continued, but by this point, I could take anything that the instructors handed out.

There is lots of travel to various training sites during Third Phase, so it went by fast. The culmination was a three-week training exercise on San Clemente Island. There we put together everything that we had been trained in to complete simulated SEAL missions. We patrolled, set up ambushes, and detonated explosives. It was everything I had dreamed of doing as a kid.

Before we knew it, graduation was upon us. By the end of BUD/S, only twenty-eight of us out the original muster of Class 237 remained. Some of our class members had been injured and were rolled into later classes. My roommate Joe and I were the only ones to share a room for the entire course without either one quitting or being rolled back.

As the candidates prepare to graduate and move forward into additional training, they're given the opportunity to indicate which SEAL Teams they'd like to be assigned to. Odd-numbered teams are based on the West Coast and even-numbered teams on the East Coast, around Virginia Beach. The elite SEAL Teams are on the East Coast, and their influence carries over to the surrounding Teams. I didn't know much about these units at the time, but I knew that ending up there was my ultimate goal. For that reason, I chose teams Two, Eight, and Four in that order, based on their reputations. I got my first choice and was assigned to SEAL Team Two.

After all that the training had put us through, graduation felt a little anticlimactic. It's a simple ceremony that takes place right on the BUD/S compound, on the same grinder where we had experienced so much pain. And it's pretty much like any other graduation ceremony: they call your name, you receive a fancy piece of paper, and some admiral shakes your hand.

The biggest change was the alteration in the temperament of the instructors. Overnight, we were treated as being part of the club. Kind of. Even though we had completed BUD/S, we weren't ready to receive our coveted Tridents just yet; just because we had graduated, didn't mean we were SEALs. Still, it was a proud moment, and I was excited for what was ahead for me. My parents made the trip to California, and it was great to see them after so many months of being immersed in the program.

▪ ▪ ▪

The next stop for candidates in the SEAL pipeline is the Army's airborne school at Fort Benning, Georgia. After a short break, we spent three weeks learning how to parachute using a static line, which deploys the canopy automatically as the jumper leaves the aircraft. Everyone there, including the instructors, knew that we had just made it through BUD/S so they pretty much left us alone, correctly assuming that there was nothing they had in store for us that we hadn't already endured in spades.

Following the Fort Benning training is SEAL Qualification Training (SQT), a three-month course on the other side of Coronado, which is designed to teach BUD/S graduates the skills they will need in the Teams.

The training is fast paced and gave advanced instruction in the basic skills that we were exposed to in BUD/S: shooting, demolitions, and diving. I loved every minute of it. This training used to take place during a six-month probation period at the respective SEAL Teams, but the standards were all over the map. Someone above had decided that a formal training course was a good idea. Our graduating class was among the first to go through SQT.

With the war in Afghanistan already underway, SQT brought an immediacy to the need to be ready for anything. I began to mentally and physically prepare myself for life on a real Team, because I assumed that I'd be deployed overseas right away. I soaked up every class and started pounding the weights really hard.

Just as I'd discovered at Quantico years earlier, I found that I had a knack for CQB. We ran through urban combat scenarios at full speed, clearing rooms and engaging targets as we went. Processing problems rapidly while moving and shooting came pretty naturally to me, and I quickly found my niche; it's been my thing ever since.

Although nearly everyone made it through SQT, a few didn't. We were out running our Zodiac inflatable boats one day when two of the boats ended up on a collision course. One guy obviously hadn't spent much time around boats, and he stuck his foot out to prevent the two craft from colliding. His ankle snapped instantly. He was rolled back into another class and, although he eventually found his way onto a Team, he got out of the Navy pretty quickly. I guess it spooked him. As he found out the hard way, nearly everything we did was dangerous, and that was with no one shooting at us.

At the end of SQT, we finally received our Tridents. It was the proudest moment of my life. The path that had led me there was long and winding, but my dreams had come true. I was a SEAL, ready to join my Team and head off to war.

I couldn't wait to check in at my Team. As I made the cross-country drive with the family, I kept my Trident inside the dashboard console. Every few minutes, I would pull out the Trident, smile, and then put it back in its place. I did that for the entire 2,700-mile journey. I ultimately gave that original Trident to my dad, who is still my personal hero, and he has it to this day.

HOT WASH

There will always be obstacles in life, but there's a solution to each one. The tough part is finding out what exactly that is. For me, it was a bathtub and a snorkel. Finding a way to address my weaknesses and build them into strengths got me through the dive phase of BUD/S. It wasn't about being tough; it was about being smart. There were times, though, where I simply had to be tough.

Night dives demonstrated how, when given the opportunity, your brain will expose all of your fears. Darkness, sharks, sea monsters, more sharks. (Did I mention sharks?) Accept the fact that you are at the mercy of the environment. Focus on the task at hand instead of dwelling on what you cannot control.

Those of us who are old enough will never forget September 11, 2001. We lost many American lives that day, and even more during the wars that followed. God bless them and their families. Out of that tragedy, though, came hope. The country stood together and acted as one. We were truly United States, a team. "United we stand, divided we fall" isn't just a catchphrase. Compared to those heady months after 9/11, we have become divided beyond belief. If we don't find a way to work as a team, we will fail as a nation.

PASSION AND PURPOSE

After driving cross country with the family, I checked in at SEAL Team Two in Little Creek, Virginia, near Virginia Beach. Team Two was one of the two original SEAL Teams created during the Kennedy administration and, because of the time difference with California, it is actually a few hours older than Team One. Those original SEALs soon found themselves in Vietnam and quickly became legendary warriors. There is a lot of history at Team Two, and I was proud beyond words to become a part of it.

I made arrangements for us to rent a house in Virginia Beach, got my family settled, and began to prepare myself for check-in day. Unlike in the Marine Corps, where I lived on base among my fellow warriors, my family and I lived together in a regular suburban neighborhood that was not unlike the one that I grew up in. My neighbors were cops, business people, teachers, and salesmen. I headed to work every morning; the only difference between me and other breadwinners there was that my job was to prepare to fight our nation's enemies—being a SEAL doesn't exempt you from the normal tasks, stresses, and activities of any other homeowner.

The first thing that happens when you check in at a Team is that you are assigned your gear. Like most SEALs, I love gear, and I was like a kid in a candy store as they handed over all of the tools of the trade: helmets, body armor, uniforms, web gear, dive gear—you name it.

Being the new guy is never fun, and there are some horror stories about the things that newly arrived SEALs are subjected to when they come aboard. It was a little different for me, though. For one, I was older than most of my BUD/S classmates, not a kid, when I showed up at the team. More importantly, I'd spent my three months at SQT hitting the weights hard: if I was going to be in a close combat environment, I wanted to be able to physically throw bad guys around. I'm five feet ten inches tall; I'd graduated BUD/S weighing 193 pounds, but by the time I made it to Team Two I had beefed up to 225. I couldn't run worth a damn, but I didn't care—I didn't plan on running away from anyone. As a result, when they started issuing me gear, the first thing they did was give me new cammies, since the ones I was still wearing were too tight. When it came to new guy hazing, I think maybe the Team Two guys looked at me bulging out of my clothes and decided they would pick on someone else.

This was an exciting time to be in the Teams, with everyone jockeying for a slot to get overseas and into the fight against those who had planned and executed the attacks on our homeland. It was only a few months after 9/11, and the war in Afghanistan was in full swing. To put it into context, the Battle of Tora Bora, where coalition forces barely missed catching Osama bin Laden, had happened only a few months prior. Operation Anaconda, one of the largest battles of the entire war and one where SEALs played a notable role, had also just taken place. After decades of relative peace, we were in an all-out war in some of the most inhospitable terrain on earth.

I've gone through life with a bad case of what I call "TOMS Disease": Terrified of Missing Shit (you could think of it as Stage 4 FOMO, Fear of Missing Out). I'm not sure what childhood event caused this condition. It has kept me out at the bars far too late, hanging around just in case something fun might happen.

In the miliary, it made me always try to be the first one to sprint through the door on a target, the risks be damned. As terrifying as war might be, my real fear was that I wouldn't get my chance to get into the fight. We had no idea that this war would last another two decades, and that a second front in the Global War on Terror would open up in Iraq within a year. Needless to say, I would get my chance. Before 9/11, SEAL Team regions of responsibility were assigned geographically, each Team with a separate region of the world. Team Two's focus historically was Europe. But by 2002, all bets were off, and every Team was a prospect for receiving orders to Central Asia or the Middle East.

Everything in the Teams, whether in peacetime or during a war, happens in a cycle. A Task Unit of SEALs is formed and begins the process of pre-deployment training, called a workup. The members train together for months in platoons or smaller, skill-specific squads and teams before the entire Task Unit deploys overseas. After the Task Unit returns from a deployment, the cycle repeats itself.

During the workup, the new guys were expected to get themselves up to speed on all of the weapons and equipment that we would be using downrange. I arrived at the beginning of a workup, which gave me the opportunity to learn as much as possible before we went to war. I wanted to build my reputation in the Teams as a capable operator, and this was my first opportunity to do that.

My experience as a Marine really allowed me to shine—I was running circles around the five or six other new guys who were doing most of these tasks for the first time. Whether it was operating a belt-fed machine gun or doing land navigation, my time as an infantryman put me ahead on the learning curve. **As in anything you do in life, experience pays off.**

As I mentioned, one of the things that attracted me to the East Coast was the influence of the nearby SEAL Teams that were the elite of the elite. Much of what this Unit did is classified, but, suffice it to say, it gets the greatest missions, the largest budgets, and uses the most cutting-edge weapons and tactics. I didn't know much about the Unit in those days, but since I was always looking for the next big challenge, I knew that I wanted to be a part of it. SEALs from the Unit commonly transfer to other East Coast Teams for a deployment or two before returning to the Unit. Two of the senior enlisted SEALs in my Task Unit had spent time at the Unit, and they helped design and implement our training program. Because of their experience and training, those men became a huge influence on me and my teammates. They changed the organization of our entire Task Unit to be like this elite Unit, with each man assigned to either an assault, mobility, or sniper team. As a result, we were far ahead of other SEAL Task Units in terms of capability.

These senior enlisted SEALS harped on CQB to the assaulters, so I spent my days doing livefire "house runs," which took my skills to an entirely new level. The veterans' kit bags had their old squadron's patch on them (the Unit is divided into squadrons, rather than platoons), and I would stare endlessly at those coveted symbols. I was determined that I would follow in their footsteps when my time came.

Since I was a bigger guy, as well as being a new guy, if we were doing anything other than house runs, I was the one stuck carrying the big machine gun. The MK43, a.k.a. "the pig," is the SEAL version of the belt-fed Vietnam-era M60. The gun itself weighs twenty-three pounds, and each box of one hundred rounds of 7.62mm ammunition weighs seven more. I usually carried five hundred rounds; you can do the math. Add in body armor, a helmet, and all of the other assorted items that I had to carry, and I was loaded down like a pack mule. It was good for me, though, and I learned to do it well. Once you get comfortable carrying a big machine gun on training ops, a regular M4 carbine feels like a feather.

I was fitting in and doing well, but I may have been a little too confident of my abilities. The senior guys quickly put me in my place. We were riding in a van one night and I was drunk—I mean *really* drunk. I must have passed out, and when I came to, I was being held down by the rest of the SEALs in the vehicle. I began to sober up instantly when I realized what was going on. They made it clear that I needed to watch my mouth—that I was still a new guy and had a lot to learn. They were right, of course, and I took their warning to heart. I needed an attitude adjustment, and they gave it to me.

There was a guy in my platoon, Darren, who had arrived at the Team one deployment cycle ahead of me. He gave me the hardest time, which was difficult to swallow since he was essentially a new guy as well. For some reason he had a chip on his shoulder, and he took it out on me. Darren reminded me of the corporal who had scolded me for my push broom skills back at Quantico. All through my first workup, Darren would give me shit relentlessly. "You're too big, Eddie, how are you going to handle the mountains in Afghanistan?" he would say.

Another time, we were in a wind tunnel practicing our freefall skills. The essential skill is to maintain stability in the air with no lateral movement that would crash you into a teammate. I mastered it quickly and decided to try some other moves. I began flying as high as I could into the tunnel before diving downward and stopping just before I hit the net below. It was not only a helluva lot of fun, it was great practice. Darren didn't approve. "You need to learn how to fly, we don't need you going up and down," he chided me. I wanted to punch him in the face.

The workup is also the time when individual SEALs head to various schools, both in and outside the Navy, to build their skills. I attended jumpmaster school, dive supervisor school, and load planner school, as well as various weapons-related courses in which I learned to maintain each gun that we used.

Two months into my time at Team Two, I was told that I was heading to Army Ranger School, located at Fort Benning, Georgia. One of the challenges of that school is food deprivation, and it is common for trainees to lose as much as forty pounds during the eightweek program. I love to eat, and I also had zero interest in losing all of my hardearned muscle just so that I could get a Ranger tab. Rangers are great people and extremely capable warriors, but if I'd wanted to be one of them, I would have joined the Army. I told my leadership that I wasn't going, and they finally relented. (Looking back, I kind of wish that I *had* gone, so that I could shut people up about how hard the Army's course is compared to BUD/S.)

        ▨   ▨   ▨

In the same way that my priorities had shifted away from the family when I started BUD/S, the Team became everything when I started at Team Two. I ate, slept, and breathed the Teams. As a husband and father, I was absent, both physically and mentally. I spent most of my time at work, and when I did come home, I was either on my gear or studying all of the new information that I was expected to master.

At the time, I believed that it was a necessary evil: we would soon be in the fight, and my focus could not waver. I realize now that it was selfish. There was no real work-life balance for me. Despite the circumstances, I did my best to maintain some normalcy at home, but in hindsight, I could have done a much better job.

As I prepared to go overseas, cracks began to appear in my marriage. It was Super Bowl Sunday in 2003, with the Tampa Bay Buccaneers taking on the Oakland Raiders in San Diego. I was a fan of some of the Buccaneers' players, including Warren Sapp and Mike Alstott, and really looked forward to watching it. My BUD/S roommate, Joe, had gone to Team Two with me, and I had him over to watch the game.

We all had a few drinks, but my wife took it to a whole different level. She became increasingly angry as the night went on; all I can assume was that she was jealous that I was paying more attention to the game and to my friend than I was to her. Her anger ultimately turned into rage, and she charged at me with a kitchen knife, while my friend watched the entire thing. I grabbed the knife and snapped off the blade.

▪   ▪   ▪

Despite the troubles at home, I pushed aside the drama and focused on preparing for war. The workup flew by, and before long, it was time to deploy.

The only problem was that our leadership wasn't really sure where they wanted to send us. By this time, the wars in both Afghanistan and Iraq were raging. Things were in flux, and the higher-ups were shuffling units around, trying to find the new normal. At first, we were told were going to Germany; there was no war in Germany, but they wanted us in Europe. It didn't make any sense, but that plan quickly changed, anyway. The next plan was to send us to South America and the Pacific—again, not places where there were wars going on.

Finally, we got word that we were headed to Mosul, Iraq, for direct-action missions. We were going to kick in doors and shoot bad guys, the exact things that I had become a SEAL to do. It was finally my time: I was headed to war.

HOT WASH

In the Teams, I quickly learned the importance of wisdom and experience. Those who came before me had a wealth of knowledge, which they shared selflessly. I learned so much from those men, and those lessons certainly saved my life time and time again. Reading or watching a video about it can only teach you so much; nothing, and I mean nothing, will ever compare with what you learn from doing it yourself. Form your own opinions by spilling your own blood, sweat, and tears, because only then will you truly understand. Until you do, listen and learn from those who have gone before you.

Guys like Darren are haters. **In school, at work, and in life, there will always be those individuals. You know you. Be you, and don't listen to negativity.**

THE REAL THING

＋

The Humvees powered their way through Mosul's deserted streets; the nighttime curfew was well into effect. We were en route to my first target, on my first operation, on my first combat deployment. After a journey that had begun in my childhood and taken me through years of preparation and training, I was finally at the show. After years of practice, it was game time.

It wasn't like you see in the movies, where guys are praying and sharpening knives on the way in; it was more like the lead-up to a parachute jump: everyone was thinking about what they needed to do. We were professionals heading to do a job.

There was always a bit of gallows humor in these situations; someone would say something like "I hope I don't get shot in the face," and we would all laugh. I was probably a little nervous but mainly excited. Most of all, I was ready.

We spent many of our nights out on direct-action missions like this one, chasing down insurgents and the last vestiges of Saddam Hussein's brutal regime. We were basically a SWAT team serving warrants: our aim was to apprehend these suspected enemies, but we were ready to kill them on a moment's notice if the need arose. Except for a handful of the older guys who may have seen some brief action in places like Bosnia, none of us had ever experienced war. We were a bunch of rookies, albeit highly trained ones, heading into a life-or-death situation.

We left a few guys with the vehicles and moved the rest of the way to the target on foot. Ordinarily, someone's first op would be standing overwatch, or maybe doing surveillance, something designed to ease you into things, as another element hit a target. This was the opposite: we were going to blow down a door and rush into a house where people were likely armed and prepared to kill us. Sure, I'd done this before, but the bad guys were always paper targets that never shot back.

We hit the target; of course, I was the first man in the door. I turned right, just as I'd done thousands of times in training, and began the methodical process of clearing the house, my weapon up and ready. The last thing you expect to encounter in that situation is someone charging directly at you, but that's exactly what happened. An adult male in white manjammies was sprinting toward us. For a brief moment, we all froze. It was probably only a fraction of a second, but it seemed like an eternity in the moment. That was the kind of indecision that can get you killed. I snapped out of it and choke-slammed the man to the ground—he was unarmed and didn't need to be shot. Behind me I heard our chief, who had served in the Unit, say, "Clear the fucking house." His message was clear: keep moving, do your job. We never had to be told that again. The rest of the assaulters snapped out of it, too, and began moving to the next room.

We did forty to fifty similar direct-action missions over the next two months, never firing a shot. The Army's special operations unit was in town, and they would get all of the juicy targets; we would get the leftovers.

It was an ideal progression, from a career standpoint: things were turned up, but just a notch or two—we were gaining valuable experience without any of us getting hurt or killed. In my mind, though, there wasn't enough action.

One night, we finally got a high-profile mission. Intelligence pointed to the location of Abu Bakr al-Baghdadi, a real bad guy, who would later command ISIS. He would become infamous for orchestrating and participating in the rape, torture, and brutal murder of civilians under the banner of the Islamic State. In those days, he was not as high profile as that, but he was known to travel with ten to fifteen armed men who were ready to fight at a moment's notice. The Army's assets couldn't get out of Baghdad due to bad weather, so the target was ours. We were pumped to have the opportunity.

Because of the heightened level of danger, we decided to land right on the target to maximize speed and surprise. We would most likely take fire immediately. We were prepped to go when the call came at the last minute, canceling the mission.

It wouldn't be until October of 2019, fifteen years and thousands of victims later, that al-Baghdadi would finally be brought to justice

during a special operations raid in Syria. With US forces closing in
and a military canine on his heels, he knew that his capture was
imminent. Al-Baghdadi fled into an underground tunnel and then
detonated a suicide vest, killing himself along with three children.

All of us were disappointed but understood that this was part
of the job. For myself, however, I realized that if I wanted to go on
these types of important missions, the premier SEAL Unit was the
place to be. This realization was one of many decision points that
would change my path forever.

Not long after that, we received orders to head to Baghdad
on a new mission: to serve as Personal Security Detail (PSD) for
the interim Iraqi government, basically acting like Secret Service
agents. Another unit protected President Ajil al-Yewer, while we
were assigned to Prime Minister Ayad Allawi.

In Iraq, the president is mainly a ceremonial figure, while the
prime minister runs the government. The insurgents saw Allawi
as a puppet of Washington, which made him an attractive target,
and so Allawi was under constant threat of attack. This wasn't
the first time that he'd ever been in danger, however—he had survived multiple assassination attempts. A former Ba'athist, Allawi
had split with the party and moved to London in 1971, where he
would pursue his education as a neurologist while in exile. Then-
Vice President Saddam Hussein had ordered Allawi's execution, and in 1978, he had been attacked in bed by an axe-wielding
assassin. Wounded and left for dead, he had spent the next year
recovering in the hospital. The scars on his head earned him our
immediate respect.

We protected Allawi 24/7, driving him around and shadowing
his every move. The entire Western world was behind us at the

time, and everyone wanted the fledgling democracy to survive. The allied nations sent their best vehicles to help us do our jobs: we had Mercedes and BMW sedans along with Ford Excursion and Explorer SUVs, all of them armored. These cars and trucks were worth a minimum of $500,000 apiece, and they were being driven by twenty-somethings who weren't exactly known for being easy on equipment.

PSD work is both boring and, at times, extremely stressful. None of us wanted this job; we'd gone from direct action, where we had the element of surprise, to basically becoming targets ourselves. We weren't really trained for this type of work, but we were fast learners.

Baghdad was my first real introduction to the improvised explosive devices (IEDs) that would plague Iraq for the next decade. Giant explosions would erupt, sending debris and shockwaves hundreds of meters in every direction. We would examine the blast sites in the aftermath and would find dozens of shoes, their owners having been blown out of them by the powerful blasts. Human bodies, almost all of them civilian, were turned into ash. The same people who did this were determined to kill Allawi and would be happy to kill a bunch of American SEALs in the process. It was pretty unnerving.

I learned a great deal during this deployment, both during our direct-action missions and while doing the PSD work. I would later apply many of those lessons learned when I started my own security company.

It was a lot of work, but it wasn't all serious. Thursday is the equivalent of Saturday in the Islamic world, which means that Thursday night is when people party. We would gather with other special operations forces from around the world, drinking and bonding with men who were working under the same stressful conditions. It blew off steam and built camaraderie. There were Americans, Brits, Australians, and South Africans in the Green Zone bars. If there was a "no alcohol" policy in Iraq, we ignored it.

During one of those nights, I ran into one of my BUD/S classmates. He had bullied one of the smaller members of our class relentlessly, smashing his painted helmet on the ground when the instructors weren't looking. I still held a grudge, and he knew exactly why. We said a few words to one another (I distinctly remember him saying "you don't like me, do you?") I have no use for bullies, whether they are insurgents who target civilians or fellow SEALs who picked on the weak. Despite my strong desire to choke him out, I walked away.

We ultimately spent four months in the Green Zone protecting Allawi, ending our six-month deployment. All in all, it was a pretty anticlimactic trip compared to what I'd looked forward to, and it was nothing like the heavy action I would see in the future. Our only casualties came from a bad traffic accident on the highway, when one of our vehicles plowed into a concrete barrier at high speed. It had been a dark night, and the driver hadn't seen the barrier until it was too late. Everyone survived, but several members of our platoon had to be sent home due to their injuries.

HOT WASH

War isn't fun. People get hurt and killed, and the civilians suffer horribly. All of that said, I'd signed up for this. I'd become a SEAL to go to war. **Keep your head in the game and remind yourself of the "why." Remember that you spent all those hours preparing to achieve your goals. Soak it up and enjoy the ride, passionately doing what you love.**

War is chaotic and confusing. As much as I love CQB, I will say that I found going into a person's house in a combat scenario to be overwhelming at first—having to process all the moving components under the surging adrenaline was simply a brain buster. Suddenly, the training pipeline made sense: as tough as it had been, it had prepared me for the unknown world of combat. The men who served before me did an amazing job of passing down experiences and wisdom for the younger generations. I hope that you will never experience war, but whatever you do in life, **share your lessons learned with the ones who are coming up after you, always.**

THE DEPLOYMENT HAMSTER WHEEL

returned home from six months in Iraq, hugged my wife and daughter, and immediately went to work preparing for my next deployment. We were experiencing what many military families, especially those in special operations, were going through at the time: the wars came first, family came second. My daughter Samantha was born; three months later, I was headed back overseas. They had called for volunteers to head to Afghanistan, and I raised my hand without hesitation—I wanted back into the fight.

Samantha had incredibly blue eyes and strawberry blond hair. She looked nothing like me, and I would joke that her father was one of my teammates, who had the same coloring. Because I was gone so much during her formative years, I didn't bond as deeply with Sammie as I had with Kailha. On the rare occasions when we were all home together and awake, Kailha would snuggle with me, and Samantha would cling to Leia. She was a mommy's girl from the start, but I loved her all the same. I hated to leave again, but this was the path that I'd chosen: my job was to go to war.

We were at the stage in our pre-deployment workup at which nearly everyone on the Team attended various schools to learn specialized skills. Before I shipped out for another taste of war, I took one of the most important steps in my career: I became a breacher. A breacher is the guy whose job it is to get the rest of the team inside the target by any means necessary. I'd always known that I wanted to be a breacher; to me it was the coolest job in the world to kick in doors, or blow them off the hinges using explosives. I had done some breaching during my first deployment, but I wasn't technically a breacher, since I had not yet attended the NSW breacher school. Now I would.

The three-week course was held at Fort Pickett, a forty-three-thousand-acre National Guard base located in rural Virginia near the tiny town of Blackstone. We started by learning about windows and doors: how they work, where the hinges are located, and all of other details needed to get into a building in a hurry. The instruction didn't dive too deeply; it was more of an exposure to each method of entry. At first, we simply mule-kicked doors with our feet, and then learned to employ simple manual tools such as a sledgehammer, a battering ram, and the "Hoolie tool" (a.k.a. a Halligan bar), which is a forcible entry tool also used in firefighting.

We then progressed to the use of quickie saws, chain saws, torches, and, finally, explosive breaching.

Once we learned the different tools, we did house run after house run, rotating who was breacher each time. Blow or otherwise breach the door, rush inside and clear the structure, and then line up and do it all over again. It was CQB all day long, and I loved it. Of all of the training schools I've been through in my career, and there have been plenty, breacher school was my favorite. I ended up graduating as "Honor Man," meaning that I was voted the top performer in my class. The prize? A free shotgun. If I had to sum up my entire military experience in one word, it would be "breacher"; that job defined me as a SEAL.

As our workup progressed, our ranks were bolstered with new SEALs just coming out of SQT. We were doing some mobility training at Fort A.P. Hill in Virginia; on this one particular day, I was lead petty officer, responsible for coordinating that day's training.

I was writing on a whiteboard when one of the chiefs came in, showing three or four new guys around. I looked up at them and nodded; at first glance I read them to be good guys who carried themselves well. You are always sizing people up in this line of work. Later, I introduced myself to them. The tallest of the group was a good-looking guy named Jason Workman. Jason was from Utah and had grown up in the Mormon religion. He was a confident, happy individual, and we connected instantly.

Jason showed an interest in breaching, and I took him under my wing to try to teach him everything that I could. Given that it was only my second platoon at the Team, I was still a relative new guy, but I enjoyed the opportunity to mentor a fellow SEAL. Very quickly, we became close friends.

Damn, he's good-looking. In Iraq at SEAL Team Two with Jason Workman,
an amazing operator and even better friend. Miss you, buddy.

▪ ▪ ▪

Before long it was time to say goodbye to the family and, once
again, go to where the bad guys were. Our Task Unit was split into
two elements: one went to Iraq, while we went to Afghanistan. I
would learn that, compared to Iraq, Afghanistan was where the
real bad dudes lived. Iraq was pretty civilized, by Western standards, while Afghanistan was a tribal culture with a centuries-
long history of warfare. Its warriors were hardened, intimately
familiar with the harsh terrain, and not afraid to die. They had
been fighting for decades and had learned essential lessons in how
to combat modern forces over the course of defeating the Soviets
and then Afghanistan's central government.

During this tour, I got my first taste of real combat. The US Army was going to be running a medical resupply convoy and asked for some of us to help fill their ranks. I jumped into the turret of the Humvee, manning the belt-fed M240 machine gun. I was accustomed to the SEAL way of doing things, which would have meant having steel ammo cans in the turret that held hundreds upon hundreds of rounds. I got behind the weapon, only to find that it had a short belt of ammo hanging from the receiver. This was not okay. I grabbed some cans of ammo from our own vehicles, so that I'd be ready for anything: I had a sneaking suspicion that it was going to be *on*.

The Afghans were wise and patient fighters. When a convoy moved up a valley, they would hold their fire and wait for the return trip. On the way back, when the personnel were tired after four days on the road, they would hit them.

This is exactly what happened to us. It was late morning and I was lounging in the turret with my helmet off, eating an MRE. We began taking fire, and one of our Afghan Army counterparts was immediately hit by an enemy round. I dropped my meal, strapped on my helmet, and started pumping full-auto fire into the area where the enemy appeared to be shooting from. Being high up in the turret gave me the best vantage point, and I directed our vehicle to maneuver to higher ground. As quickly as it began, the enemy disappeared. I felt a burst of adrenaline that was more powerful than any drug. I was hooked immediately.

Not all of the danger came from the enemy. A few weeks later another incident happened, one that I'll never forget. We were traveling in a convoy of five Humvees, passing vehicles manned by friendly forces that were heading in the opposite direction. We lost visibility in the dust cloud kicked up by the other trucks, and two of our vehicles collided, one then rolling over. My friend Adam Brown had been riding shotgun in that vehicle with his elbow on the windowsill and his hand on the edge of the roof. When the vehicle rolled, Adam's right hand was crushed. His fingers were hanging off, sliced through the bone and held in place only by the skin.

In Adam's excellent biography, *Fearless*, a medic is described as taping his fingers back on. It wasn't a medic—it was me. I had no idea what I was doing, but I put each finger back where it belonged and wrapped up the bloody mess. As it happened, I did it exactly the way it should have been done, and the doctors were able to save Adam's fingers. Despite this injury and the later loss of his right eye in a simulation-round accident, Adam went on to successfully complete the grueling selection process for the exclusive SEAL Unit, shooting left-handed to compensate for his injuries.

An FBI agent was riding in the other crashed vehicle, and the impact of the collision smashed him into something inside of the vehicle, crushing his chest. The medics on the scene actually had to cut him open and massage his heart to get it working again. He survived, but between his injuries and Adam's, it was a chaotic scene— and an eye-opener on how fast things could go seriously wrong. We hadn't even been in contact with the enemy, and yet two members of our group were on their way home with medical emergencies.

We wrapped up our two months in Afghanistan before heading to Iraq for four more months of PSD work.

▪ ▪ ▪

Jason had been in Iraq the entire time, and we'd kept in contact via email. Like me, he loved the gym, and now that I was in Iraq and stationed at the same base, we made plans to lift together every day when we could. Working out is my quiet time, and I rarely like to lift with anyone else, but Jason and I became lifting partners. We hit the weights hard, although I always teased him about his skinny legs. "They won't grow!" he'd protest. If Jason wasn't in work clothes you could always spot him in a Tshirt, flip-flops—and jeans, worn to cover up those legs.

When we weren't lifting or working, Jason and I would usually hang out together. We would eat midrats (midnight rations) together and watch more than our share of movies, usually comedies or war movies. He had a roommate, so he would usually come over to my trailer to watch *Wedding Crashers*, *300*, or whatever else was on the menu for that night.

Thursday was our night to go out to one of the various underground bars that were in the Green Zone, and Jason would come over to pregame to blow off steam before we headed out. He was a fan of the band Good Charlotte and always wanted to listen to their song "I Just Want to Live" first. It got to the point that I would have it queued up for when he walked through the door, so all I had to do was press play. He would hear it start and cheer *"Yes!"* We had some great times together on that deployment.

▨　▨　▨

Though I'd finally experienced some real combat, the deployment on the whole wasn't the action that I'd signed up for. There was plenty going on in Iraq at the time, including brutal combat in Fallujah, Ramadi, and Sadr City, but I was stuck in Baghdad, effectively babysitting and doing sniper overwatch missions. As sexy as this sounds, it wasn't all that exciting.

We would gain entry into someone's home and effectively take over. We provided security while our snipers kept an eye out for insurgents setting up IEDs. I can't imagine what those people, especially the kids, were thinking. It was strange being in someone's home, yet armed to the teeth; despite that, some of the families were very hospitable and would offer us food.

We weren't supposed to eat it, because there had been reports of families drugging Marines during similar operations; the men had supposedly been found with bullet wounds in the backs of their heads. There was one night, though, when I was so hungry that I decided to risk having my brains blown out and eat the offered food. They served me a giant bowl of rice with chicken, raisins, and grapes mixed in, along with a variety of spices. It was delicious, and I made *very* sure that no one else on our team ate it, so that if something happened to me, they could watch my back. Sometimes being the big guy on the team has its privileges.

These were important missions, but it was boring work, and even if there was any action, the snipers were the ones doing the shooting. I'm sure the general public assumes that all SEALs are doing the kinds of operations that make headlines, but that isn't really the case. I was quickly discovering that the generic Teams weren't the ones doing the things that I'd seen in movies: those exciting and high-profile missions went to the select SEAL Team.

During that trip, I happened to make friends with a SEAL who had served in the Unit, and even fought on Roberts Ridge during what became known as the Battle of Takur Ghar back in March 2002; two men had later received Medals of Honor for their heroism, one of them posthumously. My new friend was an impressive individual, and his stories only added to the intrigue of the elite SEAL Team.

Late in that deployment, this friend asked me if I was interested in trying out for that exclusive Unit through a selection process known as Selection and Training, or S&T. I told him that I'd already put in my paperwork and was scheduled to enter the process a month after we returned to the States. My plans were going to have to change when I was ordered to spend six months with a training detachment, delaying my entry into S&T. My friend must have made some calls, because the next thing I knew, I had orders to try out for the elite Unit I wanted to be a part of.

I was still in Iraq and only three weeks away from one of the toughest selection events in the world, which meant that I had to get ready *fast*. I'd been hitting the weights for the entire deployment, but I hadn't been running at all. As my deployment approached its end, I worked feverishly to get myself into shape for the ultimate test.

▪ ▪ ▪

When I arrived home I was stunned at how fast Samantha had grown. There's a big difference between a three-month-old and a nine-month-old. I had left an infant behind; while I was away, she'd become this little person. She had no memory of me and had trouble understanding why, all of a sudden, there was a man living in her house. With only two weeks before S&T, I'd barely reacquainted myself with her before it was time to leave again.

My marriage had grown increasingly volatile, and I pleaded with Leia to keep things calm while I prepared for S&T; getting ready was going to be hard enough without any distractions. I explained to her that making the cut would mean more money for our family, shorter deployments, and an altogether better life for us.

She did the exact opposite of what I was begging her for. One night I found her staggering through our house, completely out of it. I ran into the bathroom and found an empty bottle of anti-depressants; she had taken all of them at once. I rushed her to the nearby hospital, where they gave her charcoal and pumped her stomach.

It didn't end there.

There was another incident on a random weeknight; I had work the next morning. I hadn't touched a drop of alcohol; Leia, in contrast, was hammered. We got into an argument over something, and she decided that she was going to leave and take the kids with her. I was not about to let her drive drunk with our children in the car. She threatened to call the police and, angry, I broke the phone in half. She ran to the neighbors' home, where she called 911.

I don't know about the rest of the country, but in Virginia, when there is a domestic call, someone is going to jail. It seems like 99 percent of the time it is the male that is put into handcuffs, and that is exactly what happened that night. I was shocked: she was completely intoxicated and I was dead sober. Still, I was the big guy with tattoos standing out in my driveway in boxers and a tank top. I wasn't charged with anything, but they wanted me out of the house to let the situation cool off. I went to jail; my troop chief bailed me out. He had been around long enough to have seen it all and didn't seem fazed by it.

Another incident took place—one that should have been a red flag that I had brought too much of the war home with me. I went to visit my dad in Cincinnati and, as die-hard Bengals fans, we went to a game together. I drove my dad's pickup, with him in the passenger seat. Things were going smoothly until we hit a traffic jam on the way to the stadium.

Cherished moments, hanging out with my hero (Dad) at a Bengals game.

Stopping was not a part of my plan. Something snapped, and I began driving like I was back overseas. I jumped curbs, drove over medians, and weaved in and out of traffic. I would cut someone off, drive down an exit ramp, and come back up the on ramp, gaining a few yards with each move that I made. My dad's eyes were wide and his knuckles white as I drove as if I were avoiding an ambush. After six months overseas, it was impossible to flip off that intensity switch and adapt easily back into a normal life. I did my best to explain that this was how I was accustomed to driving after being overseas. I'm sure he thought that I'd lost it.

HOT WASH

After completing BUD/S and deploying with Team Two, it would have been easy for me to maintain the status quo. Trying out for the Unit opened me up for potential failure. Though some guys have injuries or family reasons for not trying out, it is the fear of failure that keeps most SEALs away from S&T. My attitude was "Bring it on—why stop now?" The fear of failure should never be what motivates your decision-making in life. I have more respect for the men that tried out and failed than those who never took the risk.

Tough as it may be, don't ever allow anything to slip ahead of family on life's priority list. Walking the line of being both a high performer at work and a great parent at home is tough. During that period of my life, I failed to maintain that balance. I couldn't control the deployments and training, but I should have placed a greater priority on family during the times when I was home. "I will spend every Sunday with my children, no matter what," should have been my attitude. Set clear expectations with your loved ones, and make a commitment to give them what time you can. Even if you can only give your family 10 percent of your time, they will recognize and appreciate that you made them a priority. **Your family is your team; work together, and always have one another's backs**.

As much as I loved going to war with my brothers, nothing, and I mean absolutely nothing, is more important than family. No dream, no goal, no desire should take that number one spot. Putting my career ahead of my marriage and children may have seemed like a necessity, but it was a mistake. The fact is that I loved being with the boys more than I loved being at home. It was all about Eddie; I was selfish.

There will be many times in your life when impactful individuals will enter your world and make it better. Jason was one of those individuals for me. He was younger and less experienced, but I still learned a ton from that man. **Get rid of your pride and think about what you can learn from others; your shit has a stench just like the rest of us.**

ORDINARY PEOPLE GET ORDINARY RESULTS

†

As the name suggests, Selection & Training (S&T) has two goals: to screen candidates for exclusive SEAL training and to provide those who are selected with the skills that they will need if they are successful. As hard as BUD/S was, I think that S&T was more difficult, both mentally and physically. S&T is a bit like the NFL Combine, in which potential pro football players are evaluated by talent scouts to determine their suitability for a team. With the exception of the very capable EOD techs in our class, we were all already SEALs with several years of experience. We had already proven that we were tough; the instructors at S&T were there to find out if we had the aptitude to operate at the highest level of special operations.

Between fifty and sixty of us showed up at the select Unit training compound to start down the path that could lead us to the pinnacle of the Naval Special Warfare community. The compound was the Navy version of the Forbidden City. For nearly all of us, the only other time we'd ever been allowed through the gates was when we had presented ourselves to the review board in our dress uniforms.

The first hurdle after arriving at the compound is the initial screening, which is essentially a physical fitness test. The test itself isn't necessarily hard, but in order to move forward, your performance has to be exceptional. Having just returned from a deployment, I didn't have much time at all to train for it. (Ever try to find a swimming pool in Iraq?)

It starts with pull-ups: candidates are expected to do a minimum of fifteen to twenty in under two minutes—if you let go of the bar, you're done. The next events are two minutes each of strict push-ups and sit-ups before a three-mile run. There aren't long breaks between the events, so the cumulative effects of the individual exercises make each successive one more difficult. Running was always my weak link, so it was the only event that I was worried about.

When the three-mile run began, my thighs were still smoked from the more than one hundred sit-ups I'd just knocked out. Two hundred twenty-five pounds of muscle is great for kicking down doors and tackling bad guys, but it isn't ideal for running. I took off at a pace that I felt I could maintain, falling in behind the fastest runners in the group. I pushed myself hard, knowing that this run was the only real barrier between me and fulfilling my dream. As we approached the finish line, I stepped on the gas and made an all-out sprint. An instructor called out our times as we crossed the line, marking each of them on a clipboard. The standard was 22:30, and I made it in 22:14.

Each event took out one or two candidates, ending their path on day one. The big weeding-out though, would be the swim.

Being a former competitive swimmer certainly put me at an advantage, but this swim was an entirely different animal than anything that I'd experienced before. Dozens of SEALs sprinted into the bay water all at the same time, pushing and shoving their way to the front of the pack. It was like a salmon run, or maybe the beginning of a triathlon. I hit the water and almost immediately got kicked in the face by someone's fin, knocking my mask askew; I cleared out the water and powered through it. I remember seeing random fins sticking out of the water that belonged to some poor classmate who'd been a victim of the full-contact start.

Soon I found my groove, kicking and stroking my way rhythmically through the water, just as I'd done in high school and during BUD/S. Things settled down as we each settled into our own pace and, unlike in the run, I was near the front of the pack when we came around the kayak that marked the halfway point of the one-mile event. I kept my pace, kicking hard to push myself over the final leg of the course. When I staggered onto the beach I was exhausted, but I knew that I'd made it. I stood on the sand and watched the remaining swimmers make their way onto the beach; at least a dozen guys were still in the water when the timer hit the cutoff. Those of us who had completed the swim on time began to loosely gather, individuals gelling into what would become a class.

Later that day we were checked into the Command and were issued ID badges since we would be sticking around, at least for a while. It is funny how proud that little plastic ID made me feel; I wasn't a part of the Unit yet, but it was a tangible symbol of my progress.

At BUD/S, the truth is that some of the instructors are turds. They get assigned there because they didn't perform in the Teams or got themselves in trouble. At S&T, the instructors are absolute pros. These were extremely experienced assaulters who had temporarily stepped out of the deployment pipeline, usually to give their families a break. We respected these men, and they treated us like adults. They were intimidating and held us to an incredibly high standard, but they weren't dicks about it.

This was an interesting time to be going through the S&T process. The men under this Command were being deployed at an extremely high pace to at least two combat zones, and several had already been killed or wounded overseas. It was sobering to walk in the footsteps of some of those giants, knowing that we would soon be in the fight. I'm sure the reality of the wars made the Unit instructors scrutinize us even more carefully since, if we made the cut, we would be the ones watching their backs.

CQB is the first major phase of training, and its completion is one of two big milestones at which many of the candidates are carefully weeded out. The first two weeks of CQB took place right on the compound, and the pace was unbearably slow. Moving through buildings with multiple armed men can be incredibly dangerous, so we literally had to learn to crawl before we could walk.

We would move slowly through the houses using our fingers as guns, like little kids playing war. Three weeks earlier I had been a SEAL in a war zone, and now they didn't trust me with a firearm. It was first one-man room entry, then two-man, slowly escalating until we moved through the rooms as a team of four. We progressed to pistols, dry-firing at the targets. Then we dry-fired with rifles, maintaining the same uncomfortably slow pace. Finally, after what seemed like an eternity, we got to use live ammunition. For a guy who loves action, it was frustrating.

Just as the pace picked up a bit, our training moved to a different site, one that I would become intimately familiar with over the next few years: a civilian-run shooting school south of Memphis, Tennessee, called Mid-South Shooting Institute. Better known as "Shaw's," it was staffed with a combination of civilian and SEAL instructors.

The pace dropped back to a crawl, because Shaw's was all live-fire. Instructors watched quietly from the catwalks above us, like all-seeing gods. Trust me when I tell you that they don't miss anything.

During live-fire training, movements are scrutinized, shot angles are measured, and every step that a trainee takes is carefully studied. The buildings, known as "shoot houses," can be reconfigured in different ways to keep the trainees on their toes: in each training round, you never know what a room is going to look like until you're through the door.

Trainees move as a carefully coordinated team, taking out targets as they clear the house. Relatively minor safety violations are considered strikes, and too many will send a trainee packing. A major safety violation will end your training right on the spot. You're done. Darren, who had given me a daily ration of shit at Team Two, made a bad shot in the house. The instructors counseled him, and yet he did the exact same thing the next time through. Darren got flustered, did it a third time, and was sent home. I watched the entire scene, dumbfounded. The instructors are looking for SEALs who can maintain their focus no matter how tired or frustrated they are.

Before long, the pace had progressed to full speed, which is when candidates really started getting cut. Ever since my days in the Marine Corps, CQB has been my comfort zone: I just "get it." Thanks to thousands of repetitions in both training and combat during my time in the Teams, my skills had advanced even further.

I don't know if it is a natural talent or the result of having had some great instructors along the way, but I have the ability to enter a room and very rapidly process what needs to be done. I quickly emerged as one of the best performers in the class. Everything in S&T is merit-based: all that matters is how good you are at your job. Besides being judged by the instructors, each of us rated our peers on a weekly basis, listing our top five and bottom five trainees.

Because of my performance at Shaw's I was quickly made a team leader, despite being somewhat junior in rank and experience. I was a first class petty officer, while all of the other team leaders were higher-ranking chief petty officers. Being promoted to team leader was unexpected, and it felt great. This was a breath of fresh air compared to my experience in the Marine Corps, where rank had been everything. In the Teams we don't get hung up on rank— we are war-fighters, and we conducted business accordingly. It is all about how well we perform our jobs.

S&T is relentless. We would show up in the morning for a "short" run that turned out to involve covering miles and miles in the middle of nowhere Mississippi. I felt like Forrest Gump. We would be fatigued from the tough morning workouts, get thirty minutes to eat, grab a quick ice bath to help our legs recover (if we were lucky), and then have to go to work the rest of the day in the shoot houses.

Your legs are Jell-O before the tactical training even begins. Unlike BUD/S, S&T was evaluating the candidates' performances under operational conditions, so we had to wear all of our gear, including our body armor, and that added to the difficulty of each task. It was exhausting.

But I didn't have much time to think about it: all I could do was focus on doing my job. **Maintaining that focus was everything.** The punishment for making a mistake in the shoot house was to run or bear crawl to a huge oak tree, where a flexible steel caving ladder hung from a high branch. The candidate had to sprint to the tree, climb the ladder in full gear, and then sprint back to the shoot house. Your body is smoked and you go right back into the stack to make another house run. Because you're physically exhausted, you're more likely to make another mistake, which sends you sprinting back to the tree. It's a cycle that you don't want to be in. The lesson is simple: don't mess up.

Another difference between BUD/S and S&T is that S&T's instructors weren't actively trying to make candidates quit; they were simply holding them to a standard—a very high one.

The pace of the training continued to pick up, and at the end of each week, each candidate would have a counseling session with the instructors. You either got a thumbs-up, a thumb-sideways, or a thumbs-down. A couple of thumbs down in a row and you were sent packing. One by one, candidates were dropped from the program because their performance wasn't up to par. I saw really good operators disappear. To me, it was all pretty mind blowing.

After we finished CQB, as we focused on land warfare, the pace slowed just a bit. This part of the course was more about making us better than weeding us out.

I was putting skills to use that I'd learned over the course of my career and was also learning new things every day. I loved it. I was part of the way through S&T and things were going great, professionally.

▪ ▪ ▪

Personally, not so much. The annual SEAL reunion takes place in Virginia Beach each summer when active and former SEALs and their families converge in what is effectively a giant family reunion. I'd never been to a SEAL reunion because I had always happened to be on deployment overseas when it was going on; I was really looking forward to spending time with my friends, old and new.

During the reunion, we were out at a bar with some other Team guys and, once again, my wife got upset. We were all talking shop, and Leia finally complained that I was ignoring her. I told her that if she wanted to be part of the conversation, she needed to join in. She responded that she was going home and stormed off.

I was carefully watching my alcohol consumption that evening, because I'd long since learned that I could not let loose with her around because something bad would happen. Sure enough, a short while later I got a call from the babysitter, telling me that something was wrong: Leia had called her and said something to the effect of "take care of the kids." There was something in her tone of voice that struck the sitter as a cry for help. I called my wife's phone and got no answer. Then I received a text message from her that said, "I'm in a hotel, you'll never find me. You're not going to have to worry about me ever again." Evidently, she intended to try to kill herself.

I methodically called every hotel in the area, asking whether she had checked in, and I found her on the fifth try. I spoke to the front desk and explained the situation. They tried to get into the room to check on her, but she had locked the door from the inside. I told them to call the cops and have them break the door down, or I'd hold the hotel responsible for Leia's death. Whatever our problems were, I wasn't going to let the mother of my children do this to herself.

The police broke the door down and found her in the bathroom, covered in blood. Blood-soaked towels littered the floor; she'd cut both of her wrists, one more severely than the other. They rushed her to the ER at the local hospital; after being examined and physically stabilized, Leia was admitted to the psych ward.

I was in the middle of one of the toughest training programs in existence, but every night after work, I would go visit her at the mental health facility. Her parents came down to watch the children while I trained; after visiting Leia each night, I would go home and relieve them. At the time, I thought to myself that this was no way to live, and it wasn't fair to me or to the kids. I couldn't focus on the mission *and* worry every day that she would take her own life.

In hindsight, the stress on Leia of taking care of the kids alone while I was gone on training trips and deployments must have been too much for her to deal with. There is a reason that special operators have such high divorce rates. I was absent mentally, physically, and emotionally, and always put my career first. I was not innocent in the collapse of our marriage, but enough was enough. I made the decision that I was going to leave her; timing was the only issue left to resolve.

▪ ▪ ▪

I needed to focus on the course. The next phase, which is also the other milestone at which candidates are dropped, was freefall parachute training. This took place outside of Tucson, Arizona.

I had been through freefall school while at Team Two and had somewhere between twenty and thirty jumps under my belt, but our exclusive Unit didn't recognize that course, so I had to do it all over again. The instructors treated us like we'd never jumped before, beginning at a very slow pace, just as they'd done during the CQB phase.

At its outset, the course was more or less a review of what I'd previously learned, and I found it pretty easy. However, the reason the Unit didn't recognize the prior training and started us over with the basics was simple. This course was in high-altitude military parachuting. There are two types of freefall jumps: HALO and HAHO. HALO stands for "High-Altitude, Low Opening" which means long freefalls from miles above the earth before the parachute is deployed. HAHO is "High-Altitude, High Opening:" the chute opens not long after exiting the aircraft, enabling the jumper to glide long distances under canopy before landing.

Both methods are tricky, very dangerous, and definitely not for everyone. Because everything in S&T is done as if it were a real mission, in this case that meant jumping into unknown drop zones in the dark, wearing night vision goggles, carrying full battle gear, and breathing oxygen from a mask because the air at altitude was so thin that we'd otherwise pass out.

We spent a lot of time training in wind tunnels to perfect our ability to "fly" as we exited the aircraft. Trainees were judged on their stability, because mid-air collisions with other jumpers can be deadly at freefall speeds. Some candidates failed because they got injured, while others didn't make it because of lack of adequate control during freefall. Adam Brown, whose fingers I'd reattached after the Humvee accident in Afghanistan, struggled with this aspect of the jump training but made it through with his characteristic determination. **He was a man who always made things happen; he had true grit**.

Once your canopy is deployed, it is all about being able to land on the "X." Doing this requires learning to fly the high-performance parachute like a hang glider, accounting for the wind and flaring the chute at the appropriate time. We jumped day and night, carrying full combat loads. We would complete the mission and then extract before planning our next op.

I was doing great, until I came down with strep throat very near the end of the course. I had a 103-degree fever and was hallucinating. I felt like I couldn't get out of bed, much less perform at the level that was expected for one of the final events in our training.

The instructors advised me that if I couldn't jump, I would be rolled back to another class. So, pumped full of antibiotics and sucking on a great-tasting cherry Luden's lozenge, I staggered onto the plane, where my teammates helped me put on my gear. I was miserable as the aircraft gained altitude; all I could think about was getting back into my bed. I didn't care whether I lived or died.

But when the time came, I threw myself out the door and into the thin air, somehow managed to maintain stability, and landed where I was supposed to. As soon as we were done, I collapsed into my bunk and slept for what seemed like days. **There is a message here: tell excuses to fuck off**.

Everyone who makes it through the freefall leg of the training will most likely graduate, and so those of who had again made the cut began to see the light at the end of the six-month tunnel.

Our very last hurdle was SERE school, run by the Air Force near Spokane, Washington. SERE stands for Survive, Evade, Resist, Escape and is designed to prepare individuals for what life would be like if they were ever captured. It is pretty much mandatory for air crews and special operators. Some of us had been through SERE training before, but this was different: while traditional SERE applies to being imprisoned by a foreign military in a World War II or Vietnam scenario, this advanced version focused on the very real threat of being captured by terrorists.

Most schools start with instruction and end with practical testing; this school was the opposite. On our first day there, they served us a big meal and encouraged us to dig in, because we wouldn't be eating again for a while. Then, with our stomachs stuffed with food, they immediately locked each of us into boxes built out of plywood. The boxes were pitch black inside, and the space was too small to either stand up or lie down in.

We were dressed in scrubs, and the only thing we were given was a coffee can, to serve as our toilet. I'm pretty claustrophobic, and knowing that I could physically break through the wood if I had to was the single thought keeping me calm.

About an hour in, a terrible smell hit me. Whether it was by design or accident, the food had given all of us the runs, and my buddy Adam had already put his coffee can to use. He managed to knock it over in the dark; wet feces seeped over into my box, which adjoined his. The smell was unbearable. We spent thirty hours in those boxes and twenty-nine of it was like being in a sewer. I didn't sleep at all.

Then they pulled us one by one out of our boxes and into inter-rogation rooms. SERE instructors are allowed to physically man-handle you as part of the course. You put your hands in your pock-ets and they slap you and shove you around—it's pretty rough. It's designed to piss you off, and it does. I was tempted to hit back, but that would have gotten me thrown out of the course, and I'd come too far to let my anger take over. They video the interrogations so that, later, they can critique your performance and show you your physical "tells."

After a week of abuse, the course transitions to a mostly class-room environment, where instructors review the events of the previous week and teach things like how to break out of handcuffs and other restraints. They had our attention after our interroga-tions, and we absorbed as much of the information as we possibly could. It was a very effective and valuable course.

The final exercise simulates what it would be like to escape from confinement. Trainees are driven to a location several miles away and dropped off with no money or identification. The assignment is to improvise and find a way to get back within the allotted time without being picked up by the local cops or roving instructors. Being the guys we were, we didn't exactly play by the rules. We used razor blades to cut slots into the soles of our shoes, where we hid cash and IDs. From the drop-off point, we took a cab to the nearest bar and got hammered. When the time was up, we came staggering into the rendezvous area carrying cases of beer. It was pretty obvious that we'd broken the rules. It was basically the last night of S&T, and my friend and I almost got thrown out of the course altogether. **Lesson learned: this is big boy stuff—control your behavior.**

Our premier Unit was separated into several smaller units, the names of which are officially classified (yet all over the internet). At the end of the course, these smaller units hold a draft to choose the trainees whom they want assigned to their team. The trainees being drafted are the guys that the drafters will later rely on in combat, so it's not a popularity contest. Each candidate is ranked in class order, which at this point in the game means something like one through fifty. There is definitely gamesmanship going on as the rankings are made, because the instructors jockey a bit to get the guys they want into their squadron.

Although they are all pretty much equal in terms of ability, each assault squad on the Unit has its own personality and culture. Ollie, an instructor who I'd become friendly with, lobbied me hard to join his squadron, which was known for having guys on the larger end of the spectrum. Like me, he was a gym rat, and he knew how to motivate me. "That's where the big boys go, Eddie," he would say.

I debated whether or not joining his squadron was the best choice for me. Part of me had my heart set on the squadron that my old task unit chief had come from—which he had recently rejoined—since he had been such a key influence in my path to a select SEAL Unit. I was later told that I had been ranked among the top ten in our class. I had my choice of squadron and was torn between two amazing options. I would have been happy with either. At the end of the day, I decided to follow in the footsteps of my old chief and was drafted into his squadron. I would be joining a unit whose storied history went back to the early 1980s ███████████ ██████████████████████ .

My path to becoming a warrior, which had started in childhood and progressed steadily over more than a decade, had finally led me to the pinnacle of special operations. I had found my home, my calling. I would be working with some of the best-trained, most-capable warriors in history. We would get the toughest missions, taking us to the most dangerous targets. It was exactly what I'd always wanted, and I was proud beyond words.

We all received our squadron assignments and headed to what is called the second deck, a place where only operators are allowed to go, to be "yarded-in" to the Command. This is an initiation ceremony of sorts in which each trainee is handed a yard glass of beer with a few shots of liquor dropped in for good measure. The beer is chugged, some short speeches are made, and it becomes a celebration. Each squadron has its own patches, and I'll never forget receiving mine: they depicted the same coveted symbol that I'd seen on my old chief's gear. Getting my patches was an even greater feeling than getting my Trident; I couldn't stop staring at them.

The credit belongs to the man who is actually in the arena, whose face is marred by dust and sweat and blood; who strives valiantly; who errs, who comes short again and again, because there is no effort without error and shortcoming; but who does actually strive to do the deeds; who at the best knows in the end the triumph of high achievement, and who at the worst, if he fails, at least fails while daring greatly, so that his place shall never be with those cold and timid souls who neither know victory nor defeat.

—Theodore Roosevelt

HOT WASH

S&T was a smoker. Though I never had a "snorkel in the bathtub" moment where I nearly didn't make it, it was challenging from beginning to end. For me, the runs were especially tough. That said, there was never a day where I doubted that I would make it through. With all humility, I was a great operator, and I knew it.

Everyone who shows up at S&T is a badass, capable of extreme physical endurance. Causing extreme physical exhaustion prior to training allows the instructors to see whether you are capable of maintaining a high level of performance under any circumstances. Tiny mistakes get people killed in combat, and the watchful eyes from the instructors are always there to catch those slip-ups. Those who didn't make the cut weren't bad guys, and they weren't bad SEALs; they just weren't what the instructors were looking for. I respect those men for trying.

Years later, I was on an operation in Afghanistan that required a grueling six-hour hike through the mountains in order to reach the target. It was so bad that some of my teammates required IVs to rehydrate them so that they could continue. The target ended up being an especially dangerous one, and our skills were put to the absolute test. One of the Puma-wearing bad guys had the upper hand on me, but I killed him with a single head shot while at a dead run. That's what it's all about. It was on that op that I truly understood why they had pushed us so hard. There was a method to the S&T mayhem. That was one of my closest brushes with death, and only the extreme nature of my training kept me alive. It was all worth it.

Most people will never go to S&T, but everyone has their own challenging moments in life. It might be a class in graduate school, or earning a professional certification; it could be taking the bar exam or becoming a doctor. My advice is to get as much information possible from those who have gone before you, and learn from their mistakes. What would they have done differently? When you decide to take on the challenge, go into it with the mindset that you will succeed no matter what. Have a clear path, and stay on it. Barriers will come up along the way; be a wrecking ball that will crash through them.

TIP OF THE SPEAR

As I checked in at the compound, it hit me that I'd finally arrived. I had climbed the ladder until I'd run out of rungs. I was in the most elite unit in the Navy, arguably in the world. This was the Super Bowl team. We had the absolute best training anywhere, access to the greatest equipment money could buy, the most support assets, and the biggest budget. In comparison, everything else that I'd done felt like the minor leagues.

If you're wondering what it's like to walk into the Team room at an elite SEAL Team for the first time, I can tell you that it was pretty damn intimidating. The room itself might be the coolest place that I've ever been, packed with relics of past combat missions. The chandeliers hanging from the ceiling are made from captured AK-47s, and mementos, including Uday and Qusay Hussein's boots, are on display. Team photos going back to the 1980s hang on the walls. The guys in the room had all been there, done that on hundreds of real-world missions.

Surprisingly, though, there was no hazing—everyone was a professional. These guys were happy to share their hard-won knowledge and mentor the new members of the squadron. It was a great environment to be in, and I fell in love with it right away.

Just because they didn't haze us didn't mean that they weren't scrutinizing our every move. We were still new guys who had yet to prove ourselves in their minds. During one of my first training operations, I had an incident that was beyond embarrassing. I made the cardinal mistake of allowing someone else to set up my breaching charge, and it failed to go off. The whole team was stacked in a line, ready to burst into the building and start taking out targets. I initiated the explosive charge and...nothing happened. It was the only time in my career that I ever had a failed breach, and it happened to be during my first week on the job, with the entire team watching. I managed to fix the charge, and completed the breach within a few seconds. It was a humbling experience, to say the least.

If becoming a SEAL had come between me and my role as a father, being at this premier SEAL Team only made it worse. My attitude was that I could lead this rock star commando life, and my wife would keep things operating at home. That mindset, and the daily rigors of my profession, put further stress on an already struggling marriage.

In my defense, I rarely went out to the bars when I was back in Virginia Beach, but that's about all that I can say that was positive about Eddie the family man in those days. Although I kept my drinking to a minimum, Leia did not. She drank every day, which often led to arguments. There was screaming, slamming of doors, and the like—not exactly an ideal environment for a child's development. I asked her to stop drinking, making a plea—that it was bad for the kids to see her that way—but it had no effect. I'm sure now that drinking was her way of coping with the daily stress of being, practically speaking, a single mom. But I didn't recognize that at the time. That day would come.

If my home life was a disaster, my professional world was everything that I'd ever dreamed of. I put my personal problems aside and dove into preparing to go overseas. In those days, each squadron took turns taking four-month deployments and then returning to Virginia Beach to prepare for the next one. When I arrived at my squadron, the guys were just coming off a deployment, which meant that I would be at the beginning of the year-long readiness cycle. The idea was to take leave—what the rest of the world calls vacation—and then begin the nine-month workup for the next deployment.

I won't get into too many specifics on the way things are organized, but squadrons are made up of assaulters and snipers. I was, of course, assigned to an assault team. Due to the types of missions we were tasked with, we needed the best gear available. Just about anything could be ordered: if we wanted it, we got it. As an assaulter, I was assigned an HK416 rifle, made by the German firm Heckler & Koch. For those of you who aren't gun nuts, think of it as a very high-quality version of the standard M4 carried by most American combat troops; it is basically the Porsche of assault rifles. Because we did so much training using nonlethal Simunition® paint rounds, we each had an identical weapon set up just for paint rounds. Armorers on the compound would customize our guns to our specific preferences and would fix any problems that came up.

We were each assigned an equipment cage, which is basically a closet where all our assigned gear is stowed. There were weapons, there was armor, there was dive gear, parachute gear, climbing gear—just about anything that you could imagine might be needed to complete a mission. We had clothing for fighting in the desert, the jungle, the mountains, and the Arctic. On at least a weekly basis, we would walk into our cage to find brand-new gear in boxes on the floor, as if Santa had dropped them off. The gear budget was noticeably higher than those of the regular SEAL Teams, and light-years beyond what I'd seen in the Marine Corps.

Each of us would show up in the mornings around 7 or 8 a.m., work out on our own or in small groups, and be ready to go to work by 10. There was no organized physical training; everyone knew the standards that needed to be met, so it was up to us how we got there. We needed a mix of body types on the team: bigger guys like me for kicking in doors, and lighter, endurance-type athletes who could move quickly in mountainous terrain. Some guys would take long runs or swims, while others would work on the free-climbing walls. As always, I mainly lifted weights.

Once the workouts were over, we would begin whatever training was scheduled for the day. Of course, we focused heavily on the types of missions that we would be conducting during our next deployment to Iraq or Afghanistan. We still had to prepare for worldwide contingencies, though, so we couldn't totally ignore other skills. We did a great deal of shooting and lots of CQB using the various ranges and shoot houses on the compound. On certain days we would do full exercises: we would parachute in, patrol to a target, conduct our assault, and then extract via helicopter. It was real-world stuff, and it prepared us very well for our jobs.

A premier SEAL Team workup isn't logistically too different from that of a traditional SEAL Team—everything is just bigger and better. Guys go off to various schools on an individual basis to learn new skills or enhance old ones. There are shooting schools, climbing schools, surveillance courses, and language programs available. Unlike for other units, which lacked the budget, other more unconventional schools were also available to us. We could learn to fly a plane, captain a ship, or anything else that could be justified as increasing our effectiveness. I was focused on becoming the best breacher that I could be, so most of my individual training was related to that role. I went through advanced breaching courses and lock-picking schools and learned how to bypass alarm systems. If I ever were to choose a life of crime, I would make a great burglar.

Once the individual-training slots were completed, our teams would come back together and prepare to work side-by-side in increasingly larger groups. Some of the things that we did were pretty mind-blowing in their scale. We would do complex missions in real urban terrain, taking over office buildings and other structures in major US cities. Local law enforcement would cordon off the area and we would conduct our operations using Sim rounds. If you were ever in Denver, Dallas, Miami, or Los Angeles and saw commandos riding on the benches of small helicopters that were weaving among the skyscrapers, they were probably us. Not only was the experience incredible from a training standpoint: it was a blast.

One of these trips found us in a major US city, where a small group of us worked with the local SWAT team. At one point we ended up doing some training at the massive football stadium where the city's NFL team plays their home games. The domed roof of the building was designed to allow light to enter the stadium, and was made from a very thin but durable synthetic material. We were running around the roof, doing flips and playing grab-ass, with only about a quarter-inch of plastic between us and a 168-foot drop. It was pretty spooky. Just a couple of years later, that same roof failed after being piled with a heavy accumulation of snow.

Later we moved inside, where the temptation to play on the field was just too much. Adam Brown climbed down onto the field and grabbed a ball. Soon, the rest of us dropped our weapons and joined him. We were throwing the ball around and running plays like a bunch of kids. Our squadron wasn't too far out from a deployment, so we were all being careful about getting injured. We knew Adam would get hurt first (that was a given), so we quickly decided that we would play until that happened. Sure enough, Adam was on the ground, clutching his knee, within minutes of us touching the field. Time to quit. When we got back to Virginia, his leg required surgery that took him out for several weeks. With his character-istic determination, Adam worked hard to make that next deploy-ment. As it turned out, he was a few weeks late joining us, but he made it to Iraq.

We were relatively small in terms of the size of our force, but we did not work alone. We deployed with support personnel from all over the military. On a given mission we might have two Air Force pararescue men with us to handle any medical emergen-cies, an Air Force CCT operator who specialized in calling in fire support, an Explosive Ordnance Disposal (EOD) tech, a dog han-dler, and other individuals. When I arrived at the Command, there were two support personnel for every SEAL; by the time I left, that number had doubled.

We also had to physically get to the targets, which often required helicopters. In both training and combat, we worked closely with the Army's 160th Special Operations Aviation Regiment, also known as the Night Stalkers. The Night Stalkers fly massive Chinooks, utilitarian Blackhawks, or the tiny Little Birds, depending on the mission. These guys are, without question, the best helo pilots and crews in the world. We could not have done our jobs without them.

■　■　■

It was pitch dark as we approached, with only the ship's lighting above visible to the naked eye. Through the lenses of our night vision goggles, the glow from the deck was nearly overpowering. Our craft moved into the larger ship's shadow swiftly and silently. The seas were rough, but at least the water temperature was tolerable. Doing this in dry suits would have made everything that much more difficult. A mix of light rain and salty waves sprayed over the bow of the cigarette-style offshore racing boat, soaking our cammies. The rough seas were about to make the next few minutes of my life exceptionally difficult and dangerous.

Our target was a civilian cruise ship; our mission was a hostage rescue. An unknown number of terrorists had taken over the vessel in international waters and were holding crew members and passengers hostage as they steered toward a hostile coastline. It was a scene reminiscent of the October 1985 hijacking of the *Achille Lauro* on the Mediterranean Sea by the Palestine Liberation Front. During that event, a wheelchair-bound American hostage was murdered and his body dumped overboard. We were here to make sure that history didn't repeat itself.

Our job was to approach the ship stealthily and eliminate the threats as rapidly as possible. This was the type of mission that led me to the military, into the SEAL Teams and, finally, to this select SEAL Unit. I was finally in the game but wasn't able to appreciate it in the moment. My team's focus was to get from the speed boat to the ship's deck, dozens of feet above our heads. (Did I mention that the cruise ship was moving at full speed?)

As the biggest guy on the team, my job was to man the extendable fiberglass pole that was designed to secure a small metal caving ladder to the ship's hull. These narrow ladders were similar to what you might see a trapeze artist climbing on. Getting the ladder connected to the ship was one of my job's toughest tasks, and everyone was relying on me. As the new guy, I really wanted to get this right. Just standing on the deck in those crashing seas was difficult enough. Add in the wet and slippery gear, the weight of the pole, and the darkness, and it became a nearly impossible task. There's a reason that not everyone is selected do this job.

The outstanding Special Warfare Combatant-Craft Crewmen (SWCCs) kept the boat as steady as possible, working the throttles on the powerful outboard engines to surf our tenmeter craft on the wake of the giant vessel above us. The rest of our team aimed their weapons nearly straight upward toward the deck, providing security while I did my thing. I braced the pole on my hip and extended it upward. The higher I held the pole, the more gravity fought against me as the boat rocked below. Raising the pole also pulled more of the ladder from its resting place on the deck, adding additional weight.

The muscles in my shoulders and arms burned as I fought the elements and the swaying weight of the pole and ladder. Our boat hit an unseen wave that sent me crashing to one knee, banging it hard on the deck. Cursing, I stood back up and got back to business. As the next wave hit, our boat lurched upward and gave me the height that I needed to secure the ladder's hook to the hull. I took a breath, pulled with everything that I had, and managed to stick it, just before our vessel crashed downward. Relieved and with throbbing hands, I collapsed the pole and grabbed the weapon that was slung behind my body to help provide cover while our climber did his thing.

The climbers were the opposite of me physically: small, light, and agile. I watched my teammate fly up the ladder like a pirate scaling a ship's rigging. I held my breath, praying that the ladder held until he could do a better job of securing it. Seconds later it was our turn to climb. Heavily laden with body armor, weapons, and assorted breaching gear, it wasn't going to be fun to scale the small, slippery rungs.

One by one, my teammates climbed up. Finally, it was just me and the boat crew on deck, and it was my turn. I looked toward the bow so that I could time the next wave. As the hull rolled over the peak, I jumped as high as I could and grabbed the ladder as the deck came surging back in my direction. Clear of the boat below, I began the fifty-foot climb toward the deck. The wind and rain bit hard as I climbed the twisting ladder, and I could feel each metal rung through the thin soles of my all-black Converse Chuck Taylors. If I slipped, I would plunge into the blackened waters below and, thanks to my heavy armor, would sink like a cannonball. Ditching my gear would be my only chance of staying alive.

Once, on a training mission, I watched with embarrassment as a ███████ SEAL officer froze while on the ladder. Whether he was fatigued or scared, I'll never know, but he eventually dropped into the ocean and had to be rescued. Though my arms still burned from manning the pole, I was determined not to be that guy and fought my way upward as quickly as possible.

Exhausted, I gripped the ship's railing and tumbled over it and onto the deck. The rest of my team was already pulling security beside me. I took a knee and scanned the ship through the twin tubes of my night vision, my infrared laser sweeping along in search of targets. After the noisy chaos of our infil, the scene was almost shockingly calm.

No words or hand signals were needed as the team rose in turn and moved quietly along the deck. We split into two teams, one heading toward an undisclosed location where they could take control of the ship. I followed my team leader toward our team's objective, the hostages, preparing mentally for how I would handle likely breach points, including doors and walls.

We have a saying in the Teams: "Don't rush to your death." Sometime during the past two decades of constant combat, we had realized that moving slowly and deliberately through a target minimizes the chance of being ambushed. All of that stealth goes out the window during a hostage rescue, though, when speed is paramount. The only objective, the team's safety be damned, is to reach the hostages as quickly as possible to prevent their captors from turning them into casualties.

The hallways and stairwells were well lit, so I moved my goggles up toward my helmet and out of my line of sight. We jogged through the labyrinth of the ship's interior, looking for the ballroom where we believed the hostages were being held. We had neither the time or the manpower to clear every passage so it was up to the last man to ensure that threats did not emerge from behind us. We hit an intersection, and my team leader glanced quickly at a diagram attached to his wrist. He turned right and we all followed close behind, our footfalls suppressed by the ship's plush carpeting.

As we approached the main ballroom, darkness abruptly fell over the ship's interior. The other team had obviously reached the engine room and cut the power. I flipped my goggles back into place and my aiming laser, invisible to my naked eye, reappeared. I checked the door, preparing to breach it, but found it unlocked.

When you go into a room in a building or a ship, you don't know whether you are walking into a tiny closet or an expansive auditorium. What you do once you're through the door will depend entirely on the situation, and the decision-making process has to be instantaneous. The four of us alternated directions as we entered, flowing smoothly and silently thanks to thousands of repetitions in training.

Over the quiet calm of the ship's interior I heard the roar of rotors above the ceiling, as helicopters from the 160th Special Operations Aviation Regiment swarmed the ship. Snipers perched in Blackhawks covered the decks with their rifles, while assaulters fast-roped down from other aircraft. MH-6 Little Bird helicopters buzzed around like lethal insects, ready to pounce. Within seconds, the size and capability of our force increased dramatically. The downside was that the bad guys would now hear us coming. There's always a tradeoff.

We came to another door and, this time, found it locked. I pulled my crowbar-like Hoolie tool from its place on the back of my armor and, within seconds, had the door flying open on its hinges. As Dom, who was our point man, made entry, I heard the code word that signaled a large room that required as many men as possible to clear. I could hear shouts and screams from within as I rushed inside the large open ballroom. We quickly formed a formation that saw all four of us clustered together with our weapons trained in various directions. I caught movement to my left and saw a weapon. I swept my laser toward the terrorist and dropped him with a quick pair of suppressed shots.

There was a mass of bodies in the room's center, which appeared to be hostiles standing over hostages who were kneeling, sitting, or lying on the carpeted deck. My teammates' weapons spoke as I searched for a new target. We closed the distance fast, and those with hostile intent became more apparent in the darkness. I pumped a half dozen rounds into two armed men standing side by side, sending them both to the ground. My muzzle found another target just as Dom fired and sent the terrorist crashing into a table. I swept left and right but found no one standing. It's common for hostiles to hide among their hostages, so I scanned the mass of panicked bodies looking for weapons or any sign of a suicide vest.

A second assault team entered through a door on the opposite side of the room and quickly joined us as we began searching every individual. Hostages were either screaming, crying, or catatonic. It was the definition of chaos. I switched on an infrared light on my helmet and began grabbing hostages and pulling them to their feet. I ran my gloved hands over their bodies, looking for guns, knives, or explosives. Given that so many people were clustered together, a single grenade would cause untold carnage. Shooting bad guys was the easy part; this was far more stressful.

"Endex!" an unseen voice called out. We lowered our weapons like boxers at the sound of the bell, and the room fell silent. The lights flickered on above us, and we each pushed our night vision googles out of the way. Everyone's posture relaxed visibly. The closest armed bad guy rose from the dead, rubbing the painful welt where the 5.56mm Simunition training round had hit his chest. He and his fellow terrorists were role players from other SEAL Teams, as were many of the hostages. This had been a carefully orchestrated and highly realistic training operation. Remember Darren, the bully from Team Two? He was one of the role players. I walked over and shook his hand. I didn't hold a grudge, and besides, I had nothing to prove. I'd made it to the Super Bowl, and he hadn't.

Someone had secured the use of an actual cruise ship for us, and we trained day and night, learning to board and clear it as fast as possible. No expense had been spared to ensure that we were ready to respond to any real-world crisis imaginable. I couldn't help but smile as I looked around the room. This is exactly how I wanted to live my life.

Our combined force all gathered in the ballroom, our bodies surging with the feel-good chemicals that follow such a high-stress event. I experienced a high that I cannot explain as our troop chief began a debrief of our team, the role-playing hostages, and the "terrorists." As I mentioned in the Author's Note, these after-action reviews, sometimes called "hot washes," were some of the most valuable learning experiences of my career.

We ran through the events of the entire exercise, covering what went well and, more importantly, what could be improved upon. Rank and seniority were invisible during these meetings, which gave everyone a chance to contribute and be heard. I listened to every word, absorbing as much information as I possibly could. Most interesting to me were the comments of the role players, since they had an entirely unique perspective. We had achieved surprise and had eliminated all hostiles without injury to the hostages. By any measure, it had been a good night.

After the hot wash, we put on dry clothes and moved to another part of the ship to eat a late-night meal. My head was still in the clouds as I dined hungrily among the finest warriors on earth. After dinner, I joined my team for a walk-through of our path from the deck to the final objective. I chimed in briefly on the topic of breaching, but otherwise stayed silent. As one of the newest members of the squadron, I was very happy not to have been called out for a mistake. I'd done my job, done it well, and was immensely proud.

My first dual breach, somewhere in Iraq.

Tomorrow we would wake up and do it all over again.

Before I knew it, it was time to go put all of this training to use. We headed out to Iraq and set up shop at the Al Asad airbase, located west of Baghdad in the infamous Anbar Province. We were attached to another element in our squadron under which we served as an assault team. That meant that I was working side by side with some of my closest friends, who happened to be on that troop.

This deployment was a dream come true for a guy like me who loves action. We would fast-rope onto targets from helicopters, blow down doors, and fight our enemies at spitting distance. Instead of firing at muzzle flashes hundreds of yards up a mountainside, I was engaging armed terrorists inside of their bedrooms.

I'll never forget my first kill. The target was a financier for al-Qaeda in Iraq, a salt-and-pepper-haired man in his fifties. It was at night, of course, and we snuck up to the target building as stealthily as possible. I could hear suppressed .45 pistol rounds going off as my teammates began to take out the sentries protecting the individual we were targeting.

It is very common for people to sleep outside in Iraq, since it's brutally hot and most homes don't have air conditioning. They would usually sleep up on the roof, but at this target, everyone slept in the home's yard. An Air Force PJ and I walked up on a sleeping couple who were oblivious to my presence. The man woke up, startled, and I watched as he reached for a handgun hidden under some clothing next to his makeshift bed. I shot and killed him without hesitation. That wasn't the strange part. His wife, who just moments before had been sleeping by his side, appeared not to react at all as her husband was killed by a man wearing night vision and clad in a strange-looking uniform. No screaming, no sobbing, no visible reaction. I took it as a sign that she knew he was a terrorist and that, sooner or later, it would catch up with him. It was as if she knew that we would come. If she was terrified, she didn't show it.

While we are on the subject, here is my honest attitude about killing: there's no sugar-coating it, it is what we do. As I advanced through increasing levels of special operations, it became clear that killing the baddest of the bad guys was the ultimate goal. If you're wondering what it felt like to take another life, I experienced only pride. These were men who tortured, raped, and murdered innocent civilians in order to increase their power and influence. People who blew up crowded markets, killing and maiming dozens without hesitation. They were the same breed that had brought so much death and destruction to our homeland on 9/11. **To rid the world of these truly evil individuals was my job, and I relished in it**. It got to the point that if I didn't kill someone on a mission, I would feel as if I'd somehow failed. I've never tried crack cocaine, but they say it's pretty addictive: I'm willing to bet that it doesn't hold a candle to the rush that comes with killing a real terrorist at close range.

There were plenty of insurgents to target in that area, and we stayed busy. We might be out five nights in a row, running ops and killing or capturing bad guys. During the day we would sleep, work out, or find other ways to pass the time. We would play video games such as *Guitar Hero*, read books, or tweak our gear. If I had any real downtime, I would work on my breaching charges, searching for ways to trim down the weight of my explosive charges. There would be an occasional break in the action for bad weather, but during that entire deployment we never went more than four days without going on a mission. We also never knew when a last-minute op might pop up, meaning that we could never truly relax. If nothing was going on that night, I would lift weights a second time before showering, grabbing dinner (which was actually breakfast), and going to bed. Our living arrangements weren't the Ritz, but they were far better than a foxhole. During most of my deployments, including this one, I had my own room, which the Seabees had built for us out of plywood; we lived pretty comfortably.

We went on dozens of ops and, most of the time, there was shooting going on. These weren't random operations; we would know exactly whom we were targeting. Intelligence gathered during each night's mission would be exploited by specialists, who would use sophisticated methods to build us the next stack of targets to hit. Hitting what we called Medium Value Targets (MVTs) would lead you to High Value Targets (HVTs). Little by little, night by night, we were dismantling one of the most brutal insurgencies in history.

The deployment flew by, and soon it was time to head back to Virginia Beach, where my chaotic home life awaited me. I wanted to see my girls, of course, but I wasn't looking forward to the constant drama that was my marriage. We stayed in touch using email or Skype; things would be good for a while and then inevitably fall apart. Shame on me, but the fact is that I was so focused on work that I lost sight of the importance of my family. My wife and I actually got along better during my deployments because I wasn't around; it was when I'd come home that things got miserable. I knew that I wanted to divorce her eventually, but, because of the kids, I wasn't quite ready to pull the trigger.

Our homecomings weren't something that you would see in the movies. There was no flag waving or patriotic music. We would usually land in the middle of the night, and our tired families would be waiting to greet us. I hugged my wife and daughters and realized how much they had grown in the months that I'd been away. All of the responsibilities that I'd pushed aside came flowing back.

Coming home is strange. One night you're shooting insurgents wielding AKs and wearing suicide vests, and then, 48 hours later, you're taking out the garbage can in a quiet suburban neighborhood. Instead of driving through a trash-laden street looking for IEDs, there are suddenly school kids in the crosswalk to watch out for. There's definitely an adjustment period as you ease back into normal life, and the truth is that things are never really as they were before. **I was physically present, but emotionally unavailable.** There's a scene in the movie *American Sniper* that captures this perfectly: Bradley Cooper is staring intently at the television in his living room, beer in hand. The camera pans to the TV screen, and you realize that it's not even turned on. **Your body is home, but your mind is still overseas.**

To get through the hardest journey we need only take one step at a time, but we must keep on stepping.

—Chinese Proverb

HOT WASH

Becoming an assaulter in the Unit was a childhood dream achieved. It was the prize that I'd had my eye on for my entire life. I went from being the little kid at his first baseball game, carrying his glove in hopes of catching a homerun ball, to being the player on the field hitting that homer. I'd barely even seen the ocean as a kid, and now I was racing across it in a speedboat, armed to the teeth. I did my best to step back and soak in the moment, genuinely appreciating the experience. Honestly, it was the greatest feeling on earth. I had found and ultimately achieved my purpose.

It took a great deal of work to get there, and the leap from civilian to Tier 1 operator may have seemed insurmountable. The reality is that it took a series of baby steps to get from one to the other. There was the swim team, boot camp, the school of infantry, BUD/S, and S&T. Each was a challenge, but I didn't tackle them all at once. Nothing in life is too difficult if you break it down into small enough segments. When someone tells Keith Wood, my co-writer, that they "could never write a book," his response is usually "Can you write a page? A chapter?"

Stop and think about *your* purpose. Write it down. Is it truly what drives you, or is it what others want for you? Whatever your purpose, your goal, view each step in achieving it as an opportunity rather than an obstacle. Instead of thinking "I have to take calculus to get into medical school," look at it as "I get to learn calculus." Your life will be improved and fulfilled as you move closer to the end.

Along the way, take in the moment. Take in the people, the tastes, the smells, the sights. Put your phone down and be in your life. (If you're reading this book on your phone, by all means keep staring at your phone.)

The road never ends, and that's a good thing. There is always an opportunity to improve, to grow. This growth can be personal, professional, or spiritual. I've made it; how can I help others grow as well? Though I had a feeling of accomplishment when I got to my squadron, I still had further goals. I wanted to be the team breacher, then troop breacher, then master breacher, then command master breacher. Never stop, and enjoy life along the way.

KILL ADDICT

The next few deployments are a bit of a blur for me. Come home, see the family, complete the workup, and get back into the fight. I loved being overseas, doing real-world ops, and would count down the days until we got back on the C-17s to head downrange. Being in combat was everything to me. Night after night, target after target, I would initiate the breaching charge and sprint toward the door. The violent blast would take the door off its hinges, the debris would fall, and I would be in the room, taking out bad guys. It was the biggest rush of my life, and there is simply no substitute for that level of action.

Afghanistan is, in many ways, a tougher place to work than Iraq. This starts with terrain. Iraq is relatively flat and lies at low altitude, while Afghanistan is high and rugged; the highest point in Iraq is probably the lowest in Afghanistan. The mountains there are so high that, in many areas, larger helicopters must be used for transportation, because they have the power to fly over the peaks. Larger helicopters make bigger targets, so flying was always spooky. Flying was also unnerving because on the ground, I had control, but in the air, I was at the mercy of the pilots and maintenance crews that kept the giant machines flying.

Why walk when you can drive? Enjoying the view in sunny Afghanistan.

Helicopters are loud, which means that, unless you have a headset plugged in and are communicating with the crew, there is no talking. It's usually dark, it's often hot, and there's lots of time to reflect on your own mortality. Helicopter insertions were probably the only times that I ever sat back and thought about how dangerous the work we were doing was. My mind often went to dark places. *Would we get shot out of the sky? Would we be cut down by enemy fire as we ran down the ramp? Would I get blown up by a suicide bomber at the target?* There were so many unknowns; so much that could go wrong. My thoughts always migrated to my family, to my children. Is this where my story ends? I would be proud to die for my country; that's what I signed up to do. But I didn't want my children to grow up without a father. Would they even remember me? I felt the guilt of all of the birthdays and holidays that I'd missed, and of all of the times when I was too busy to spend time with them. I would think about that time when I should have gone out and thrown the ball with my kids. I came to realize that time is our most precious commodity; helicopter insertions were a tangible reminder that I didn't know how much of it I had left. It was a heavy burden.

The flying itself was dangerous, as well. Airplanes have wings and want to fly, but helicopters are trying their best to fall out of the sky at all times. We would be cruising along and, all of a sudden, the engines would simply quit. We would plunge hundreds of feet, sure that we were going to crash into a mountain any second. Then, miraculously, the engines would restart and we were back on our way. I always tried to push the thought of death from my conscious mind as we neared the target. Too much thinking and hesitation will get you killed. My best tool for focusing on the mission ahead was the iPod Shuffle clipped to my gear. I would slide the little white earbuds in and crank up the heavy metal. I'd look over schematics of the target building and think about what I would do when we landed. You might say that Mötley Crüe got me through some of the toughest times over there.

The eyes say it all.

All these thoughts of mortality got me thinking about God for the first time in my life. Was he real? I simply didn't know enough about religion to have a real opinion on it. Knowing that my buddy Adam was a devout Christian, I would ask him little questions about his faith. He was always patient and methodical, explaining things without trying to force anything on me. You could say that his words planted seeds that would sprout much later on. In the midst of near-constant battle, I wasn't ready for deep reflection.

The pace was relentless. We worked closely with Army Rangers, who often acted as our blocking force during operations—those guys watched our backs and did it well. Though we and the Rangers represented a tiny percentage of the nearly one hundred thousand US troops deployed to Afghanistan during the peak years of the war, we conducted 80 percent of the offensive operations. Everyone had a role to play, and ours was taking the fight to the enemy where he slept. We would go out on Christmas or on New Year's Eve; it didn't matter.

There has not been a major terrorist attack at home since 9/11, and I feel very strongly that much of that is due to our efforts overseas. Our attitude was that we would fight them "over there" so that we did not have to fight them back home. We are never going to stop terrorism, but if we don't confront that enemy and keep them on their backs where they live, they are going to hit us at home even harder. Our nation's inaction in the 1990s led to deaths of thousands of innocent Americans in 2001. We didn't intend to let history repeat itself. Countless terror attacks have been prevented or thwarted by our efforts, as well as by the efforts of our intelligence and law enforcement agencies. If we do our jobs correctly, you'll never hear about them on the news.

I've been asked whether our actions created more terrorists than we killed. That is a good question, but impossible to quantify. The lack of emotion that families would show us when we were killing or capturing their patriarch was, to me, a sign of how these men had treated their families. Afghanistan practices a far stronger brand of Islam than most of Iraq; it felt as if we'd climbed into a time machine and had gone back a thousand years. Women were treated very poorly: beaten, forced to wear burqas, and not allowed to read or listen to music.

The young children acted like any young kids would: scared, shy, or curious. But the older kids would look at us with a stare that said, "I am going to kill you someday," and we knew that they represented the next generation of terrorists. I hoped that my kids would never be fighting their kids over here or, worse, fighting them on our soil.

As I've said before, another difference between operating in Afghanistan versus Iraq was that the Afghan enemy fighters were generally tougher. Tougher living conditions, not to mention decades of near-constant war, makes for a hard culture.

In addition to the local warriors, foreign fighters would flood in from all over the Islamic world (I've heard Afghanistan described as being like Woodstock for terrorists). The majority were probably from Pakistan, but you'd see guys with red or even blond hair, which usually meant they were from places like Chechnya. These men were ready and willing to die for the chance of killing us. The terrorists would be trained in Pakistan and would make their way into Afghanistan in hopes of killing Americans. The graduation present in those training camps was often a pair of Puma or Nike tennis shoes that would enable the terrorists to move quickly through the rough terrain. If you saw a guy wearing a new pair of sneakers, he was fresh from training and was usually very dangerous.

Though it would have been easy to dismiss our enemy as primitive, they were in many ways incredibly savvy. Our intelligence indicated that the foreign fighters would concentrate their forces wherever the Western media was focused, to maximize their exposure. Their objective was to terrorize, and the media coverage allowed them to do so on a global scale.

We did a lot of vehicle interdiction in Afghanistan. Those were some of the rare occasions when we would work during daylight hours. This was far riskier, because we lost many of our technological advantages. We would wait for our all-source intelligence to ping, and when they did, we would sprint onto the Army birds and race to intercept them. We would fly above the target vehicles and our snipers would disable the motors. We assaulters would then land and swarm the crippled trucks, killing or capturing the occupants. The work was fast paced and violent.

We hit plenty of static targets, as well. Our teams would take turns, one as the primary assault team while the other maintained blocking positions, usually on the opposite side of a target.

On one night, we were the secondary team, which meant that we couldn't see much of the action out front. The assault team's entry was bogged down for some reason, and they found themselves more or less pinned down. My troop was taking effective fire from snipers and machine gun positions, both in and on the target building. It was a bad situation, and sooner or later, someone was going to get hit. I didn't like us not having the upper hand, and I decided to do something about it.

Going through a door is one of the most dangerous things you can do during CQB; we called them "fatal funnels." Someone decided that the solution was to put a massive charge on the wall and blow a hole in it large enough that going through a door would become irrelevant. It was a great solution, but the problem was that these charges weighed twenty pounds, which meant that we never actually carried them on ops. Another breacher and I worked on making the charge light enough so that it would be a reasonable load to carry on ops. I experimented with different shapes and combinations and finally came up with an effective charge that weighed only a pound and a half. It was a game-changer and is probably my greatest and most lasting contribution to my profession.

A thermobaric grenade is a hand grenade made without shrapnel. The size of a baseball, it gives you the blast without the fragmentation. With this new charge, I could blow a hole roughly the size of a basketball in a target building and then toss in a thermobaric grenade, which would usually collapse the wall. You could drive a Volkswagen through the new opening. I decided that I was going to blow our way into the building to relieve the team out front. My buddy Dom covered me while I put my charge on the wall and made a hole for us. We entered the first room to find a very surprised (but unwounded) donkey staring at us as if to say "what in the hell was that?"

The next room we entered was a kitchen, which we quickly cleared before blowing down the next wall. This room was filled with piles of grenades and enemy fighters manning machine gun positions. We quickly shot those still-armed men who weren't already dead from the blast and moved into the final room. I blew the wall down, and as I secured the room, I noticed that it had some of the softest carpet that I'd ever walked on. This was a glorified mud hut, I thought, and it had luxurious rugs like it was one of Saddam Hussein's palaces; I'd been in hundreds of houses in Iraq and Afghanistan, and I'd never seen one with carpet like this. It was only when the target was secure that we turned on our headlamps and I realized that the "carpet" was an enemy fighter who'd been blown flat by my charge. Morbid, but as a breacher, it was quite the achievement.

Later on that trip, there was another memorable use of thermobarics. We had chased a group of insurgents into a compound made up of several buildings inside a high wall. Thanks to all of the activity, we'd lost the element of surprise, and they now had the upper hand as defenders behind cover. The threat of house-borne improvised explosive devices (HBIEDs) was constant, so any time that we could cause damage from a distance, it was a good thing. As we entered the compound I threw a grenade like a baseball, and it sailed through the window of one of the mud-and-concrete buildings. When it went off, the entire section of the building collapsed. I told everyone to give me their thermobaric grenades—I had a plan to clear the target safely. One by one, I tossed grenades into the building's openings, collapsing each room like a house of cards and likely crushing any enemy fighters inside.

We finally moved to a section of the building that was constructed of reinforced concrete, which I knew I couldn't collapse with a thermobaric grenade. I switched to a fragmentation grenade and tossed it through the door. It exploded in a cloud of dust and I rushed inside, my teammates right behind me. I saw a man with a weapon and fired, dropping him immediately. I came around the corner and found a second armed enemy kneeling behind a couch. He was so close that my muzzle was touching his head when the gun went off; his head exploded. A third fighter popped up and I shot him down; he dropped instantly. Within the space of ten or so seconds, I had killed three men as if they were cardboard targets. I emerged from the building, covered in dust from all of the explosions. Like all of us, I was just happy to be alive.

On another vehicle interdiction op, we landed at sundown. Due to the transition between daylight and darkness, I could still see, so my night-vision goggles were hinged up onto my helmet. One of the target vehicles was in flames, which would have washed out my night vision anyway. I ran up to the driver's side door and saw Rocket Propelled Grenades (RPGs) inside the vehicle. I shot the driver through the window and he exploded—my bullet probably hit a grenade that was hidden on his body. I had no eye protection on, and the metal shrapnel hit me in the face, narrowly missing my eyeball. It was a reminder of the ever-present danger of what we were doing. I can still feel that chunk of metal beneath my skin today.

In some cases, especially when we were running dry of targets, we made a conscious effort to take the enemy alive so that they could be interrogated. Probably because I was big, scary-looking, and covered in tattoos, I was the designated battlefield interrogator. When we took a target alive, the interpreter and I would pull them into a room and see what we could learn from them. I'm sure we scared the hell out of them, but we didn't do anything that was out of bounds. Those interrogations led to other targets, which meant more enemies that were killed or captured. It didn't take us long to secure the region.

With things more or less settled in that area, we moved down to a base located in Afghanistan's most dangerous province. We began operating in an area that was totally controlled by our enemy, with the goal of clearing it of hostiles. Our operations switched from vehicle interdictions to hitting target buildings where the bad guys slept. We came in the night, slowly dismantling their leadership structure, just as we had done elsewhere. We hit them hard.

The Afghans thought that the squadron patches that we wore depicted a wolf (they didn't), and so we quickly earned the name "Night Wolves" among the local population. We heard terrified radio transmissions warning that the Night Wolves were coming. It gave us a psychological advantage that we exploited as best we could. During a thirty-day period, we cleared the area of all terrorist activity, and things stayed quiet for an entire year after we rotated out. It was great to have made a tangible difference in the lives of the local population by rendering the area safe.

We were constantly experimenting with new weapons and gear to keep our edge. For a while I carried a small submachine gun called an MP7 that was much lighter than my rifle. It fired a tiny little bullet and, with a suppressor attached, it was almost completely silent. It appealed to me since, as a breacher, I was always looking for ways to lighten my load. There is always a trade-off, though. One night I shot a terrorist through the abdomen with dozens of rounds and put another into his eye socket with it. He had taken what should have been numerous lethal hits and was still breathing. That kind of thing could get you killed, so I ditched the little gun and went back to the proven HK416.

Later, the killing became so routine that we progressed toward increasingly difficult means to keep it interesting. When shooting

bad guys with the rifle got old, I relished in the opportunity to justifiably use a pistol or even a knife when the situation permitted.
In hindsight, it was reckless to not use the most effective weapon
possible on every mission to ensure that I made it home safely, but
that was not my attitude in the midst of war. You go to a different
place when you're in that kind of combat on a daily basis. If you've
never experienced it, you'll never understand.

In hindsight, all of the killing certainly took its toll on me.
Having friends killed was even worse. I would return home from
deployments and look at civilians with disgust. My attitude was
that "these people have no clue what the world is really like." The
fact was that a small percentage of us were fighting and dying
every single day, while things back home were running as normal.
It wasn't their fault—they didn't sign up to fight, and I did—but that
wasn't the way I looked at it at the time. Given what I viewed as
their sense of unjust entitlement, I was bitter.

I was also selfish. When everyone treats you like you're special,
it is inevitable that you start to believe it. As I saw it, I could do no
wrong at home. I was sick of my wife, and she was sick of me. I
would roll in like the celebrity dad, do fun things with my kids, and
leave the mundane grind of parenting to Leia. I was checked out of
the marriage. She asked me to go to counseling, but I refused; as
far as I was concerned, she was 100 percent of the problem.

HOT WASH

I never wanted to die, but during those heavy moments when I had time to reflect upon my own mortality, I was content with the idea of dying at any moment, knowing that my children could be proud of me. The way that I saw it, a warrior's death would be a fitting end to my story. This attitude wasn't based in any spiritual beliefs, because they didn't exist at the time. I was simply doing what I loved with the men I treasured, and if it all ended there, so be it. I didn't want to die, of course, but I had made my peace.

We Americans are blessed to live in a country that is safe and stable. Bad things happen here but, for the most part, those responsible are held to account. That is not the case everywhere. Real evil exists, and in much of the developing world, evil reigns. Terrorists and insurgents operate by instilling fear among the local population. It was a great feeling to go into one of the most dangerous areas on earth and render it safe for its civilians. We made a tangible impact that I am proud of.

I hope that no one reading this will ever be forced to take another human life, but there are times when it becomes necessary. The men that I killed were the epitome of evil, and sending them to their maker made the world a better place. I'm not ashamed to say that I've never felt more alive than when I was causing death. I killed many of those real-life monsters with zeal. Do I regret taking so many lives? The answer is no. If I have any regrets, they surround the shots that I didn't take—the shots that could have saved lives. More on that in the next chapter.

IF THEY ARE WILLING TO DIE

onths later we were back in Iraq, taking on a more determined enemy than we'd faced last time I was in-country. It was during this trip when, for the first time, I experienced some remorse for killing someone on a target. I entered a room and a man reached for an AK. I shot him without hesitation, and he died immediately. For some reason, though, it felt strange. I began to question whether I could have taken him alive. I won't go as far as calling it guilt, but that kill didn't sit well with me. I asked one of our intelligence analysts to let me know what he could find out about this individual, hoping for something that would erase my self-doubt.

I didn't have to wait long. The analyst already had the video cued up when I walked into the room (it was from a CD-ROM or hard drive that we had recovered at the target). He pressed play, and there on the screen I immediately saw the man that I'd killed that night. The camera panned to a group of men on the roadside who were tied to stakes in the ground, their hands bound behind their backs. The prisoners were civilian contractors: truck drivers from places like the Philippines who had risked their lives in a dangerous overseas role simply to provide for their families. They had no dog in this fight. They had been captured when their convoy had been ambushed and, unarmed, their very existence hung in the balance. One by one, the man in the video approached and shot or stabbed the innocent workers. He didn't merely execute them, either; he shot or cut them in different places on their bodies to see how they would react. He was using truck drivers as ballistic testing dummies. Those images changed my perspective completely; never again would I hesitate to kill one of our targets. These were evil men who didn't deserve to live.

Then, a few weeks later, something happened that changed my entire perspective on life and death.

It was after 10 p.m., and the desert sun had retreated from the sky, casting the urban landscape in a cool darkness. Baqubah is a city of half a million people, situated thirty miles northeast of Baghdad. The night was quiet, save for the occasional barking dog in the distance. The permanent smell of trash and human waste filled the air. The temperatures were in the 60s, but even so I was sweating, thanks to the heavy body armor, assorted weapons, and other gear that I was carrying on me.

I was part of a group of twenty, made up of my fellow SEALs, support personnel, and one canine, patrolling toward our night's objective: kill or capture a high-value target I'll call "Z." Z was reportedly part of a group of Hussein-era special operations troops who were involved with a suicide attack network; this network extended throughout Iraq's Diyala Province. He and his cohorts were responsible for countless deaths and were believed to be working directly with al-Qaeda leadership.

We moved through the abandoned streets swiftly but quietly, since the element of surprise was one of the few advantages that we had over the enemy. My team leader was sick and was unable to go with us on the mission, which meant that I would serve in that role. I scanned the scene through my night vision goggles, confident that each highly experienced man on my team would be doing his job.

We kept "vampire hours" during these deployments: sleeping during the day and working at night, when our technology gave us the greatest tactical advantage over the enemy. Army troops had moved us most of the six kilometers from our temporary head-quarters toward the target using Bradley armored fighting vehicles, and we had then moved the rest of the way on foot.

Though we all had numerous combat deployments and count-less hours of training behind us, no one rested easy. We were out like this most nights, taking the fight to the enemy and gathering intelligence that would lead us to our next night's target. We would hit an objective, exploit the information, and strike again. Rinse and repeat, night after night. Little by little, we were eliminating in Iraq the brutal elements of al-Qaeda, a terrorist movement that later famously evolved into ISIS. This cell was the exception to the rule when it came to the fighting spirit of the Iraqis: they were lethal.

This was my fifth combat deployment as a SEAL and my third as an operator at our SEAL Unit. Though such missions were routine for us, there was no room for complacency. The squadron that we had replaced had lost one of their men to a landmine a month before our arrival. Just four days earlier, another team of SEALs from our squadron approached a similar target on a kill/capture mission; the enemy knew that were being hunted, and they made the decision to blow themselves up using HBIEDs rather than being taken alive.

I was covering the main assault team when it happened. I was standing on a stool that I'd improvised from rubble so that I could look over the stone wall toward the target building. I could see an adult male inside the house through my night vision; I was fifty yards away at the most. He was shirtless, clad only in a pair of pants. I didn't see any obvious sign of a weapon, but I could tell that he had something around his body. Could it be a suicide vest? Our team's EOD tech had killed a bad guy just a few days before who'd been wearing an explosive belt. He warned us all that this cell of fighters were ready and willing to die.

From my vantage point I watched through the doorway, pointing my IR laser at the individual who, I assumed, was our primary target. My first instinct was to kill him, but his lack of a weapon gave me pause. Within seconds, he gathered several of his young children around him and initiated his explosive belt, killing himself as well as the women and children inside the structure. As if in slow motion, I could actually see the roof of the building rise up above the walls before it settled back down. I was blown off my perch and onto the rubble below. I had just watched a man murder his entire family in a flash.

*The price of freedom. Dom and I paying respect to a
fallen brother before a mission in Iraq, 2008.*

On that same op, my friends Nate Hardy and Mike Koch were
killed by enemy machine gun fire as they were clearing a small
structure to apprehend their target. They threw grenades into
the room before they cleared it, but the enemy was in a fortified

position. Both were hit in the doorway as they entered; one died immediately, while the other lived only a few more minutes as the medics worked furiously to save him. We'd had a Super Bowl party planned for that night, but we'd gotten called out on that mission instead. By the time we'd returned to our base, those two amazing men had left this earth.

Just before this deployment was when Adam had hurt his leg playing football in the NFL stadium. That injury had kept him home for a few weeks, which meant that he was there to deliver the news to Nate's widow. He comforted her and handled the logistics of his funeral, making sure that everything was just right. In hindsight, I can't help but wonder whether his injury was pure serendipity or part of some master plan.

We still had work to do, so the Army sent two of their own special operators to fill our ranks for the remainder of the deployment; those guys were absolute pros and fit right in. That night, as we approached our objective, we knew that we faced the new threat, HBIEDs, along with every other danger one could encounter when fighting a determined enemy on their own urban turf. Every window or rooftop could conceal a sniper, every piece of trash on the street could be hiding an IED. We were the best-trained troops in the world, though, armed with the latest and greatest weapons and gear. Deadly AH-64 Apache attack helicopters loitered overhead to provide us air support if needed. We were a small but lethal group.

We were not to be the primary entry team on the operation that night, which meant that we would split up our four-man fire team to provide cover while the others moved inside. As we approached the target, snipers from our Recce element moved to nearby rooftops to provide overwatch protection while we took our positions around the two-story concrete and brick target building. I was paired up with Luis Souffront, the same Explosive Ordnance Disposal (EOD) expert who warned us about the explosive belts just days earlier. Luis and I had met during the grueling six-month selection and training process for our command and quickly became close friends. In those days, EOD men endured the training right alongside SEALs, and Luis turned out to be the best shooter in our class. Luis was effectively a SEAL and EOD combined and was a lot of awesomeness wrapped into one human being. A first-generation American and the son of immigrants from the Dominican Republic, Luis had grown up in a working-class family that earned everything that they had. His work ethic, no doubt instilled by his parents, was an inspiration to all of us. Luis put me to shame.

Luis Souffront, one of the greatest warriors that I ever had the pleasure to serve with. He was the walking definition of a "legend."

I was covering the front door of the target building, and Luis was to my left, around the corner of a low wall. The masonry wall provided us with good situational awareness: it was fifteen yards from the front door and about four feet high, which offered great cover while still leaving good observation of the target area. The main assault team was positioned to my right behind the wall, standing by to move to the front door and make entry. Since these insurgents were known for using explosives, we were going to do everything very methodically and avoid entering the building if at all possible until everyone was outside.

Our interpreters, whom we called 'terps, yelled in Arabic to the people in the house to open the doors and come out showing their hands. After a few shouts, the front door opened and a bewildered man in a white robe stood looking out into the pitch-black night, where we waited to pounce. Instantly, a dozen infrared laser aiming dots appeared on his head—if he made a sudden movement, we would kill him without hesitation. The man at the door of the target building and our 'terp exchanged words, and the man stepped outside so that he could lift his manjammies and show us that he had no weapons concealed under the garment. Our 'terp then asked for all the people in the house to come outside and do the same, so we could determine that they were unarmed before we could move them to a secure location to search them thoroughly.

A group of women and children moved toward the door but remained inside, clogging up the planned exodus from the building. When there were women and children on a target, our standard protocol was to move them outside so that we could deal with the men, but we weren't having much luck getting them to come out. Those of us who could see inside could tell that there was a commotion among the occupants of the home, and the situation rapidly deteriorated into chaos. The 'terp did his best to call the crowd outside, but with little effect.

The process was taking too long, which forced the commander on scene to change the plan. The primary assault element would move to the front of the house and pull the occupants outside so that they could be searched. Minutes went by, but the stalemate continued—we had lost the element of surprise. One of our guys spotted an armed enemy combatant inside the house and took him out. Women and children were stepping over his fallen body as they exited the building and moved toward the street. The scene was surreal.

I knew that we would need Luis to help search the individuals as they came out, given his explosives expertise. I called him over the radio and asked him to move to the front door so that he could assist the assault team in clearing the individuals from the entrance and allow them to enter the building. "Roger that," Luis said, hopping over the wall. Without hesitation, he moved into position and went to work.

One of my personality traits is that I always want to be the first one to the door; it is part of my TOMS Disease. I saw Luis move up to a huge pillar supporting the overhang that completely covered the house's front porch area, which was about seven yards away from the front door. I could tell that Luis needed help, so I moved forward and took a position right next to him. We quietly and deliberately started going over our plan of attack to de-escalate the craziness that was developing in the doorway. After a few words, I did a scan of the outside area and saw that too many of us were in the courtyard—one grenade or IED could take out several of us at once.

While I was evaluating the situation, something incredibly strange happened. A voice inside me told me that I needed to move away immediately. It was like someone was screaming for me to leave that position. It wasn't a little voice, but a booming bullhorn. It's not like me to be away from the action, but the power of that voice was too strong. It was as if some unseen force physically moved me. A tingling feeling ran through my entire body—it was indescribable.

With my left hand on his right shoulder, I told Luis that I was going to move back around to the front gate and asked him if he was okay. He said, "I got this," and I told him that I loved him. "I love you too, buddy," he responded. I moved toward the front gate to my original position and, just as I was about to round the corner, the entire house erupted in a violent explosion. The wall that we had been stacked up against simply evaporated, and the roof collapsed. For a second, time seemed to stand still. Debris blew past me as if in slow motion, and a brick hit the back of my helmet. There was dust everywhere—I couldn't see anything. Chaos set in. We had lost two men just days before, putting everyone on edge, and now this. Random gunshots rang out in the darkness. It was a total disaster.

As the dust settled, I moved quickly back toward the house and into the courtyard to see whether anyone needed help, and I felt something grab my foot. It was Digo, our Malinois canine, who was severely injured and was covered in rubble from the blast. Only his mouth protruded from the bricks and chunks of concrete, and he'd latched onto the first thing that came by, which was my foot. There was no time to help him, so I ripped my Merrill hiking boot from his mouth, probably removing a few of his teeth in the process.

I could hear the moans and screams of my teammates, so I knew that many of them had been wounded. I ran to where I thought

Luis was and found a scene that was entirely different from the one that I had just left: the whole building was gone. The front of the structure had collapsed, and the courtyard was covered with debris. The bodies of my teammates were strewn everywhere, some covered in building materials and lying still, while others writhed in stunned agony, trying to get their bearings in order to stay in the fight.

I found Luis and reached in to try and extricate his body from the giant concrete slab that covered him. I crawled under the slab, which was held slightly off the ground by some unseen object, probably his helmet. I grabbed Luis' leg and felt Jell-O; his entire bone structure had been pulverized by the blast and falling rubble. My friend's body was shattered. We quickly determined that he had been killed instantly. Where Luis had been moments before, only a body remained.

There was no time to pause and mourn his passage; we had several wounded men and work to do. What was left of Luis was pinned under a three-thousand-pound slab of concrete, and we could not move him. Fortunately, we had Air Force pararescue men, better known as "PJs," with us that carried SAVA inflatable lifting bags for situations like this. PJs are the best combat medics in the military and are amazing at what they do. These heroes are fighters and lifesavers alike. They worked quickly and efficiently to raise the slab and free Luis' remains.

With the PJs at work, I moved to my friend Benny, Digo's handler; he had fractures in both femurs. We carried him outside and loaded him into a Bradley fighting vehicle, part of the Army's quick reaction force, which was there to extract us from the target and had moved up to the buildings following the explosion. One by one, we recovered our wounded, loading them into the vehicles so that we could move away from the target.

Luis was dead, and several other men were badly wounded: a fractured spine, a broken pelvis, collapsed lungs, compound fractures, and traumatic brain injuries. Digo was alive, but critically injured. The bodies of our enemies were strewn about the courtyard, one of them thrown fifteen feet by the blast. After a half hour that seemed like an eternity, we had finally loaded everyone into the convoy and were able to begin our move to safety.

Given the combination of the concussion of the explosion, the brick to the head, and the shock of losing one of my closest friends, the ride back to our compound was a blur. We had been blown up twice in one week by suicidal enemies. For the first time in my life, I was experiencing the "fog of war."

Back at the compound, no one said a word as we offloaded the vehicles and headed back to our respective rooms. My friend and roommate Dom and I sat on our beds and just looked at one another with blank faces, tears welling up in our eyes. All we could do was shake our heads. I finally had a moment to reflect on Luis' death, and I thought about what an amazing operator and friend he had been. I could not get over the fact that I should have been buried right next to him, having been there not even ten seconds before the blast. I felt hate and regret toward myself for telling him to go to the front door in the first place. I asked myself, "If I had never said that to him, would he still be here?" To this day, the thought haunts me; I have a hard time shaking it off.

Our normally active compound stood in virtual silence for days. We all handle events such as these differently, something that became evident during the hours and days after Luis' death. Some men would sleep for what seemed like days, while others couldn't sleep at all. I would sleep for a couple of hours and then wake up in a daze. I couldn't read, watch TV, or even play video games; I would just walk around like a zombie before crashing again to catch a few more hours' sleep.

Three days after we returned, we held a simple memorial ceremony to say goodbye to Luis. The SEALs and support personnel stood in ranks in front of Luis' battered helmet, rifle, and boots. The gear was placed on a small wooden base with the rifle's muzzle pointed downward and the helmet resting on the stock. We would keep these makeshift memorials erected for the rest of each deployment so that they stood as a reminder of our fallen teammates. Luis' memorial stood next to Mike's and Nate's, erected inside our courtyard just a week earlier. The chaplain said a few words and a handful of us spoke.

It is easy to believe that you are invincible in this business. After enduring so much training and surviving multiple deployments without any of your friends falling to the enemy, such thinking is unavoidable. We had the best training, the best equipment, and fought with every advantage that we could. But now, here we were, with three men killed and several more wounded within the span of a few days. Our myth of immortality was shattered. The insurgents in this cell were willing to die without hesitation, taking as many of us with them as possible. How do you defend yourself against an enemy that has no fear of dying?

It was a strange, deeply unfamiliar time. But we still had weeks left on our deployment and more targets to hit every night. We were several men down from the explosion, so SEALs were sent from various postings around the globe to backfill our ranks.

Adam joined us as well. Within a few days we were going back out, hunting bad guys. I would be lying if I said there wasn't a bit of hesitation in all of us. We all moved more slowly and deliberately, trying to be as cautious as possible while still doing our jobs.

Over the past several years I had grown to hate our enemies and relished wiping them from the earth. I had seen the brutal acts that they'd committed against their fellow citizens and felt no empathy for them or their cause. After losing Nate, Mike, and Luis, my desire to kill grew even stronger. I shifted all of my feelings toward ending their existence. I became obsessed. I couldn't bring my friends back, but I could avenge their deaths, one bad guy at a time.

When this nightmare deployment finally came to an end, we took the opportunity to give Luis a fitting memorial. We had a special stone marker made to honor him, and a group of us traveled down to Miami to visit with his family. Luis was an avid spearfisherman, and we made the decision to set the carved stone on the ocean floor in one of his favorite spots. Luis' family stayed on the boat as we took the stone to the bottom, diving in the same waters that Luis had been so passionate about.

Each February, around the time of Luis' death, we make a pilgrimage back to South Florida to visit Luis' undersea memorial. We dive down and look for the marker, and then relax on the boat with Luis' father and uncles, drinking beers and telling stories about him. Afterward, the family prepares an enormous meal for us in their home. Aunts, uncles, and cousins all gather to celebrate Luis' life on this earth. It is a special time for those who loved Luis the most, his family and teammates alike. I'm not always able to make the trip, but every time that I do, I feel comfort surrounded by Luis' home and loved ones.

TOP: *Each year we dive in Luis' favorite spearfishing spot. Through his family and friends, his memory lives on.* BOTTOM: *Dom and me paying respect to our friend, Luis with the love of his life, Jami.*

HOT WASH

Reading this chapter brings back visceral memories of the night when Luis was killed. Tears stream down my cheeks every time I read or discuss it. The survivor's guilt is overwhelming, and I get emotional every time I think about it. It was as if we were on that operation just last week—I can smell the debris and feel the choking dust pouring into my nostrils as the concussive force of the explosion waned. I can hear the cries of the wounded men and can feel Luis' shattered flesh under the concrete.

Follow your gut. Always listen to that inner voice. Learn to discern the good voice from the bad, but always stick to what your gut tells you: it will save your life. I didn't realize it at the time, but that inner voice that saved my life was unimpeachable evidence that God is real. I don't know what his plan is for me, but he wasn't ready to let me go that night. I still question why I heard that voice and Luis did not. Why me? Why him? I won't know the answer in this lifetime.

Never stop evolving. When our actions became predictable, our enemy gained an advantage and good men died. Keep learning, keep changing, keep adapting.

More brains are better than one. Like all combat operations, this one was a team effort. Luis was covering the door, poised to clear individuals as they moved from the house. The dog and dog handler were doing their work while the snipers covered us from overwatch positions. When the building collapsed, the PJs sprang into action and worked their magic to treat the wounded, free Luis' body, and allow us to exfil safely. Concentrate on teamwork and apply it whenever you can. If nothing else, it's more enjoyable to go through life surrounded by good people.

Life is precious. Enjoy, love, and cherish the time with your friends, your family, and your colleagues. Learn from each other. Tell stories that highlight people's best attributes, and celebrate those around you. Tell your friends and family how you feel about them. As much as Luis' death pains me to this day, telling him that I loved him in that moment gives me some comfort. It can all end fast, and there's no pain worse than regret.

The men and women who serve this country do so with honor and pride. They suffer, so that you won't. Always cherish their willingness to sacrifice, as well as the sacrifices of their families.

SHATTERED

The same technology that broadcast the wars in Iraq and Afghanistan across the world also gave us a means of staying in touch with our families. We had daily access to email and Skype, so staying in touch was far less of a challenge than it had been for servicepeople in our nation's previous wars. I would email just about every day to let everyone know that I was okay, but I only used Skype a couple of times per week so that I could see the kids' faces. How well I stayed in touch depended on my mood and, honestly, I often just wanted to be left alone.

When you're overseas, your life is simple and orderly. Everything but the mission is put on hold. There are no bills to pay, you don't have to get the oil changed on your car, you're not worried about what you're going to make for dinner, and the constant task of maintaining a home and a yard is nonexistent. All that matters is staying alive. So I'll admit that I wasn't always interested in hearing about stuff back home like the toilet backing up, or a light bulb being out, when just hours before I'd been in a close-range gunfight. I did want to hear about my kids' lives, see their new pets, and find out how school was going, but I still usually needed some time to decompress before I checked in. The dichotomy of our lives could be overwhelming.

Although drinking is not officially allowed during deployments, it is pretty common among special operations forces. It was a way to unwind and decompress on the rare night when we didn't have to be ready to fight at a moment's notice. After losing Nate, Mike, and Luis on our previous deployment, though, I stopped drinking altogether. My therapy had always been lifting weights, and I hit the gym twice a day for the remainder of that trip. I was all business, but lifting gave me time to reflect on my life, whereas drinking just let me shove my thoughts into a bottle.

翼　翼　翼

Things at home were getting worse and worse. As time went on, we'd had even less in common and had grown further and further apart. Even though our girls were both in school and we were living on a military salary, Leia refused to work; she would stay at home all day, which sometimes led her to drink. On those occasions, she would turn violent when I got home from work. One night, she punched the wall so hard that she broke her hand. After Leia made multiple suicide attempts, I began to build my escape plan; I'd had enough death in my life without facing the prospect of it at home.

It was an incredibly toxic environment that I didn't want in my life, and I certainly didn't want my children to be in it. I hated to break up the marriage and disrupt my kids' home, but things had become unsustainable. Her addiction and mental health issues were taking a toll on all of us. I couldn't take it anymore.

I was on my fourth deployment with my Unit when I made the final decision that I would file for divorce when I returned stateside. I lined up a place for myself to live and had all of the little details worked out.

A month into my deployment, those plans came to a screeching halt. During a Skype conversation, my wife gave me the news that she was pregnant again. Given her substance abuse and instability, not to mention the condition of our marriage, I urged her to have an abortion. She refused. I was stuck. So much for getting out. I had no intention of leaving my family with a baby on the way, so I resolved to focus my energy on making things work.

Once I was back home, though, making things work was easier said than done. After a few months, it became obvious that our relationship was too far gone and, begrudgingly, I left home and moved in with some friends from the Teams.

I was away on a stateside training trip when the Navy called to tell me that my son had been born prematurely, due to my wife's drug and alcohol abuse while pregnant. He weighed just over three pounds and would spend the first six weeks of his life in the neonatal intensive care unit. They sampled his stool and found that it contained THC that my wife had used. I was irate.

I made it to the hospital shortly after his birth and saw my son, Triston, for the first time. He was unbelievably tiny. He was inside a transparent incubator, with life-sustaining plastic hoses running from his fragile limbs and face. There wasn't much that I could do except look at him through the glass. I couldn't bear the thought of seeing my wife there at the hospital, so I mostly stayed away. Then and now, I cannot believe that I had suggested ending his life before it could really begin. Thank God, as the song says, for unanswered prayers.

She and the kids were living in the house that we owned together in Virginia Beach, and I was staying with my buddies. My life settled into a routine in which I would take the older kids to dinner and then drop them back off and head home. As usual, I was away nearly all of the time, training and preparing for my next deployment to Afghanistan, Iraq, or some other craphole in the Middle East. As usual, work helped keep my mind off the disaster that was my home life.

When I couldn't see the kids, I would always try to speak to them on the phone. I would usually hear Leia whispering to them, coaching them on what to say to me and filling their heads with lies. She was doing everything that she could to cause me as much pain as possible, with the end goal of extorting every dollar from me that she could. I began taping each phone call with the children to put her meddling on the record for the judge to see.

After six weeks in the NICU, Triston was released from the hospital. I was happy that he was on his way to becoming a healthy child, but I also knew that my opportunities to see him would now depend on my wife, since I could no longer just drop in to visit. I filed the papers to begin the process of a divorce, and each of us lawyered-up.

She had asked for my consent to move the family to Memphis, Tennessee, where she had family, so that she could get help with the baby and attend college. This was a tough decision to make, but I wanted her to get on her feet, get a good job, and be a role model for the kids. I cautiously agreed, so long as I could see the children whenever I was in the area. (The standard every-other-weekend arrangement would have been impossible under the circumstances.) I asked that she respect my right as a father and allow me to see the kids when I could make it work.

The Unit did a great deal of training at Shaw's, the same facility where we'd done much of our training during S&T. Shaw's is only a half hour south of Memphis, in northern Mississippi. It would be easy for me to visit the kids regularly. Because of this, and because it also made sense for her to have family support, we agreed to the arrangement that she'd requested.

▨   ▨   ▨

As soon as they moved, though, it was complete radio silence. Leia wouldn't let me speak to the kids on the phone, Skype with them, or even send them texts—I was totally cut off from my family. This was not what I'd agreed to. Not being able to visit or even communicate with my children was a living nightmare.

On the one occasion that I saw my children during this time, I drove six hours from Tulsa, Oklahoma, to take them to lunch, only to be told that if I didn't have them back in two hours she would call the police. Those types of interactions with law enforcement weren't exactly encouraged in my line of work, and she knew it. We had lunch, I said goodbye to the children, and I drove six more hours home.

Having dinner with my girls as my marriage unraveled.
A dark time for all of us but we got through it as a team.

The first thing that I needed to do was get the house ready to sell. Without three children, I simply didn't need the room, and it was too far from work to be practical. I had begun the process of cleaning and painting the house when my pager went off, interrupting those plans and sending me on my way to the Horn of Africa, on the real-world mission where we began this story. I called the realtor on my way into work and told him not to show the house because it wasn't ready to sell.

It was a short but successful trip; during a heliborne vehicle interdiction, we took out one of the most wanted men in the world along with his bodyguards. Minutes later we had the al-Qaeda men in body bags, waiting for our ride home.

I returned home from Africa a few weeks later, but was again kept from having any contact with my children. It was killing me to not know what was going on in their lives. I reached out to a private investigator to see whether he could help me confirm their well-being. After speaking with the PI, though, I realized that the price tag associated with that service was something I could not afford on my Navy salary. I decided to handle things myself; after all, surveillance was part of my skillset.

On my next trip to Memphis I brought along some extra gear, including night vision goggles and some recording devices, to try to get the answers I needed. My plan was to stake out the house to get license plate numbers, so that I could run background checks to see who was around my kids. I got what I needed one night and did my due diligence to put the pieces of the puzzle together. I determined that my wife was up to no good, surrounding herself with people that I didn't want anywhere near my children.

I met with my lawyer and explained that the situation was untenable—I had to be able to at least speak with my family. All I wanted was for things to go to back to our own version of normal. My attorney petitioned the judge in Virginia to compel my wife to return to the area and resume our previous arrangement. The judge set a hearing date.

Members of our unit were not clean-cut due to the nature of our work. On the appointed day, I arrived in court looking a bit like the caveman from the Geico commercial. I wore a suit and did my best to make myself look presentable, but with my long, patchy beard and unkempt hair, I'm sure that I didn't make a great impression.

My wife made an impassioned and eloquent speech, letting the judge know just how bad a person I was. According to her testimony, I'd caused her to drink and to do drugs, and was solely responsible for all of her problems. She told the judge that, without my negative influence, she was clean and sober. She should have won an Academy Award for her performance.

I remember sitting there while she was on the stand and thinking about how disgusted I was, listening to her paint this picture based on so many lies. I wanted to stop the conversation and yell, "That's not true!" but I knew that would not work in my favor. So I sat there and listened to her testimony, trying my best to contain myself.

When it was my turn to speak, I told the judge that I just wanted to be able to see my kids on a regular basis and to return to our previous arrangement. I didn't want money, or the home, at all. I offered to pay the mortgage on the house for my soon-to-be ex-wife, and pay her a healthy sum of money monthly just to get my kids back. I offered to step away from the squadron and take an S&T instructor position, which would keep me from traveling and allow me to take a more active role as a father. As difficult as it would be for me personally, I was willing to step away from my career in order to do what I had to do to see my kids.

As I was saying this, I felt as though the walls of my world were closing down around me as I mentally walked away from my dream job. You don't volunteer for careers like this unless you're 100 percent dedicated, and that's what I was. I did not want to stop until I got to the pinnacle of the SPECOPS (special operations) community, and I had many more future deployments that I wanted to complete. All I wanted was to rid this earth of bad guys and defend this great nation of ours.

My dreams seemed to be disappearing in the blink of an eye, though, and I felt lost. But I had a choice: to walk away from my career or walk away from my kids. At the end of the day, it was that simple. As much as it pained me, I knew I would be doing the right thing as a father to quit the job.

The chances of the judge doing much in my favor were slim. On one hand, he had a loving mother who'd been victimized by her husband while, on the other, there stood a shady-looking SEAL who shot people for a living and spent almost no time at home.

At the end of the hearing, the judge told my wife to go back to Memphis and continue to live with her parents—but she had to allow me to see and speak to my children when I was available. He'd bought her version of the events, but I had one card left to play: I suspected that my wife was using, and so I'd asked my lawyer that morning to request that the judge drug test us both. I knew that I was clean, and I had at least some chance that she would test positive. Leia swore to the judge that she was clean, but there was a pause in her voice, and I knew that she was lying. At the judge's order, she provided a urine sample after the hearing.

As I left the courthouse, I did my best to put the hearing behind me, focusing instead on the mission ahead. I was two weeks out from traveling to Khost, Afghanistan, to take over what we called an outstation. My job would be to coordinate with other agencies, friendly Afghan military units, and the locals to build target packages for the main body of SEALs from my team. Running an outstation was a stepping stone to reaching my goal of becoming a team leader. It was an important job, and I was focused intently on earning it. I pushed aside my problems at home and dug in to prepare.

Just two days after the hearing, I was at work when I received a text from my lawyer. I stepped out into a stairwell and called her immediately. As I'd suspected, my wife was using and had tested positive for illegal drugs. Her credibility was shattered—everything she'd said to the judge was now thrown aside. The judge granted our request and ordered her to return to Virginia Beach with the children. When she refused, her lawyer fired her as a client, and the judge told my lawyer that the kids were mine.

I was two weeks away from going overseas, and I suddenly had sole custody of three children.

"You've got your kids. Go get your kids," my attorney told me. I was stunned. I blurted out a question that, in hindsight, sounds ridiculous. "Can I go on my deployment first?" I asked. "No Eddie," she said, "you can't."

I was overjoyed, but completely overwhelmed by the turn of events. I felt like a lost child at a carnival—the entire world was spinning around me. In an instant, I'd transformed from an experienced special operator, focused on a job that I knew and loved, to a single father of three kids, one of them still a baby—a task that I was totally unprepared for.

I had to break the news to my bosses that I wasn't going to be able to deploy. They'd been kept informed of my custody situation but, like me, they hadn't expected the judge to rule in my favor. Who would? Nevertheless, they were completely supportive. My master chief told me in no uncertain terms to go take care of my family.

My Command and the men above me were exceedingly generous in taking care of me during this challenging period: they gave me two months off, no questions asked.

I learned a valuable lesson from all this: you may think you can do it all alone, but there will come a day when you'll need your family, friends, and coworkers in your corner to get you through the tough times. It is important to take care of the people around you and support them in the way that you would want to be supported. **Doing the right thing isn't always easy, but it's always right.**

I called my mother for help, and she and my stepfather, God bless them, drove down to Memphis to meet me. Leia cried, asking me, "Why are you doing this?" as her mother screamed profanities, making what was an already chaotic emotional scene even worse for our children. Her father was as cool and even keeled as always. We packed up my ten-year-old daughter, Kailha, my five-year-old daughter, Samantha, and my ten-month-old son, Triston, into my Toyota pickup. Kailha came along willingly, but Sammie clung tightly to her mother. Triston had no idea what was going on, and his eyes went wide as I strapped him into the car seat.

Overnight, I had become the children's father *and* mother. I didn't even know how to properly change a diaper. My wife and I had been separated nearly the entire time since my youngest son was born, so I'd had very little interaction with him as a baby. To say that I was unprepared would be a gross understatement.

HOT WASH

Relationships can be incredibly challenging. You should always work to improve and sustain a meaningful relationship, particularly when there are children involved. If things become irreparably toxic, however, it is often better to end it and remain cordial for the sake of your sanity and your children.

Years later, I recognize that I played my own part in the failure of my marriage. I was selfish, emotionally shut off, and mostly absent. My behavior no doubt fed Leia's mental illness and drove her further into the darkness. Take ownership of your words and actions, and don't shift the blame to make yourself feel innocent.

The fact that I even considered abortion disgusts me. Life is a precious gift from God and should be protected at all costs. To my son Triston: you have changed my life for the better and helped make me the man that I am today—I am thankful for you every day.

To my girls: you stepped up and showed amazing resilience during that tough time in my life. **I couldn't have done it without you, we did it together...as a team.**

A FATHER LOST

We weren't even out of Tennessee when I got a taste of how chaotic my life would be in the coming months. An hour into our trip I pulled into a Cracker Barrel to have breakfast, and we stood in the store area, waiting to be seated. I was holding Triston, and he began screaming. I was a stranger to him, and he had no idea why I'd taken him from his mother and the only home that he'd known. He wouldn't stop screaming, no matter what I did, and it was finally too much. I loaded the family back into the truck and found us a drive-through.

We made the rest of the fifteen-hour trip from Memphis to Virginia Beach straight through. Thankfully, Triston slept most of the way, which kept his screaming and crying to a minimum.

After a long and tiring drive, my kids and I pulled up to a nearly empty house and began the process of rebuilding a home.

When the call had come to go get my children, there had been no furniture remaining in the house, except for my bed. There were no dishes or kitchen utensils, and the refrigerator and pantry were completely bare. Each child had a single bag of clothing. There were no birth certificates, no Social Security cards, and no instructions. I would have to start over from scratch.

Once back in Virginia, I traded my beloved Toyota Tundra pickup for a used Yukon XL SUV and became Mr. Mom. (I still had my pride and refused to drive a minivan.) It was the worst and the best time of my life. My career was on hold—at best—and my teammates had to go overseas without me, but I will be forever grateful for the time that I was able to spend raising and bonding with my children.

My mom helped me, both financially and logistically, so that we could create something that resembled normalcy for the kids as quickly as possible. With my mother staying to help out for a couple of weeks, I was able to get things more or less stabilized. We stocked the pantry with food and bought all of the necessities so that we would be able to survive as a family. That was my goal: to keep us all alive until I could figure this out. (I'll never forget the first time that I headed to the grocery store with the kids. It struck me that I didn't even know what they ate—I had to ask them for their help. I had no idea what size diapers to buy for Triston, or whether he ate baby food. It was one of those moments where I helplessly looked around for the responsible adult, and then realized that person was me.)

During those first few weeks of my new life situation, one of my early SEAL mentors, a master chief from SEAL Team Two, spotted me in Dick's Sporting Goods. I had all three kids with me, Triston riding in the shopping cart and the other two walking alongside as we shopped. The seasoned veteran who had seen it all took one look at me and just shook his head. **I'd gone through some incredible challenges during my 20-year military career, but learning how being a dad turned out to be the toughest job yet**.

BUD/S is tough, and S&T is possibly tougher yet, but neither can hold a candle to the unending stress of being a single parent— especially one who is totally unqualified for the job when starting

The son that taught me to be a father. His smile made it all worthwhile.

out. You get most of the nights and weekends off during training, but never as a father or mother. Learning to change a diaper was relatively easy; not everything was.

I could rig a breaching charge that would blow a door off the hinges without hurting the person behind it, but, for the life of me, I could not get pigtails to align. Every attempt that I made to fix my daughters' hair was a failure. The only time that my girls' hair looked good was on "crazy hair day." The day that I learned to pull each half of a ponytail in the opposite direction to cinch up the rubber band, it felt like a monumental achievement. All of that knot tying in BUD/S had finally paid off.

Fortunately, Kailha was old enough to dress herself and do her own hair; she soon took over responsibility for Sammie. I spent most of my time with Triston, since he was at such a needy age, especially given his extremely premature birth. The girls were fantastic and quickly stepped up to help me. Everyone was forced to grow up faster than normal.

One day, I left Triston in his crib for a few moments while I went to the bathroom. I'd been applying Vaseline to his sensitive skin, and I unwittingly left the diaper bag within his reach. By the time I came back, the entire oversized tub of jelly was empty: Vaseline covered Triston from head to toe and was smeared over every visible surface of the crib and adjacent changing table. It took me hours to clean up the mess—but I can say with pride that he never got a single diaper rash on my watch.

At first, I assumed that most of the life that I'd known previously was over. Working out, which had always been my favorite therapy for body and mind, would have to wait. You would think that a father of three would understand that gyms have childcare facilities. Not me, so when I figured that out I was overjoyed. On most days, you could find me walking into the gym, pushing a stroller and carrying a diaper bag, with two crooked-pony-tailed girls in tow. I got my beloved workouts in, keeping myself sane as a result.

We settled into a routine and began to live as a family, but it wasn't all roses at first. Kailha and I had built a close bond when she was young, but the same wasn't true with Sammie: because of training and deployments, I had not been home much during her earliest years. The only way that I can describe her reaction to me in those days was "cold." I would give her a hug and she would go through the motions, but there was no real exchange; it was almost as if she was hugging a distant cousin.

At first, I thought that I was just too much of a stranger to her; but, eventually, I learned that wasn't the problem. She had been programmed practically since birth to think that her father was a bad person, and it would take a long, long time for her to decide otherwise. Today we are as close as can be, but it took lots of work to gain her trust.

When I realized that my kids were still being fed anti-Eddie propaganda by their mother on a regular basis, I installed a landline telephone connected to a computer so that I could record every phone call. What seemed like a state-of-the-art setup at the time seems antiquated now, but it served its purpose: I used this evidence to secure a court order to prevent Leia from filling the children's heads full of negativity. And it worked.

As I spent more and more time with my children, I became fascinated by how different each of them could be. Kailha has a great sense of humor and was generally a happy child; she and I have very similar personalities. Her favorite show in those days was *The Bear in the Big Blue House*, which seemed to play on a constant loop on our television. The two of us would snuggle on the couch watching Bear, who, appropriately enough, served as a caretaker of sorts for the other characters in the series.

Sammie, who prefers to be called Samantha unless you know her well, is my little athlete. She is fiercely competitive, no matter the sport. We were playing Wiffle ball in our backyard one day, about a year after I got custody of the kids. I warned her not to stand inside the baseline because other players could run through her, but she didn't budge. So she was in the way when it was my turn to run the bases and, true to my word, I checked her. (No, there was not much to prove by a 230-pound SEAL throwing his shoulder at his six-year-old daughter.) She went flying across the yard. But instead of crying, she quietly dusted herself off with a giant grin on her face and got right back to her base. She isn't scared of anything, which has led to more than a couple of injuries. If one of my kids was going to get hurt, it was going to be Sammie. She's had more than her share of stitches. Looking back on my own childhood, I don't have to wonder where that fearless attitude came from.

Triston is my little buddy. He was less than a year old when he came to live with me, and I've raised him ever since. I was essentially his father and mother, and because of that we have a very special relationship: he quickly became my constant companion. He wanted to be just like his dad. His first pair of shoes were black and white Converse Chuck Taylor sneakers, which have always been one of my favorites. At twelve now, he's a cool kid and has become the master of one-liners: he won't say a word for a long time and then, all of a sudden, he comes up with a zinger that has everyone in stitches. He's always been thin (especially early, when his growth had not overcome his premature birth,) but if you set a photo of me as a kid side by side with one of him now, we look like brothers.

All that I knew about parenthood was based on my own child-hood, and I reached back into my old favorites to keep the kids entertained. Besides sports and family walks, there was lots of hide-and-go-seek in the dark and various other games. I'd also do things like put on my wetsuit, mask, and snorkel and sneak into the room while the kids were watching a movie. I'd leap in front of them and roar, making them all giggle with surprise.

Our lives started to settle into a somewhat normal routine. I would wake up, make everyone's breakfast and lunches, and take the girls to their respective schools. Of course, there's the morn-ing when I was driving them and five-year-old Sammie fed baby Triston a gummy worm. He immediately began to choke on it, and I had to yank the car off the road, climb into the backseat, and clear his airway. Never a dull moment.

When Triston was still very young, he and I would spend the day at home together, and I'd do my best to keep him entertained. As any single parent knows, this is a stressful grind. My anxiety level would increase every day when it was time to pick up the kids. It wasn't that I didn't want to see them; I honestly just didn't know what to do with them—I was scared. It seemed like there was no end to my responsibilities.

In the afternoon, I would pick the girls back up, we would all head to the gym, and then back home for homework and playtime while I made everyone dinner. Spaghetti was one of the few dishes that I knew how to make. We ate it so often back then that it has become a joke in our family.

Though it seemed like I was in pure survival mode for that first year, there were times when I was able to sit back and enjoy the moment. Bottle-feeding Triston was always special. Feeling the rising and falling of his tiny chest pressed against my own as he fed and slept was like magic. There were fewer quiet moments when all three kids were home, but every so often, amid the chaos, I could sit back and look at my children as they sat on the couch with me. All content, all safe, all with Dad.

But it was only when they were in bed that I finally had some quiet moments to myself. When you're part of something like our SEAL Unit, it is all about you: what you need to prepare for the mission is everything; nothing else seems to matter. Now, it was all about the kids. It was an enormous adjustment for me, and I became lost. Depression set in, and I started drinking again. First it was just a glass of red wine every night to help unwind. That quickly became a bottle or two every evening; fearful of what the next day would bring, I'd get myself comfortably numb before going to bed and repeating the cycle once again.

While I was playing Mr. Mom, my teammates were at war in Afghanistan. After years of becoming an expert warrior and part of the ultimate warrior culture, I was on the outside looking in. It was incredibly hard not being there, missing the action and not sure how they were doing. It wasn't just that I was worried about my teammates—they were big boys who could take care of themselves. The honest truth is that I'm an adrenaline junkie, and I was missing out on the action. It was a selfish attitude, but that was my reality at that stage of my life.

I was in bed one night when the phone rang at 1:30 a.m. I knew before I answered that it wasn't going to be good news. The call was from my team leader, who was temporarily stateside for a surgical procedure. He broke the news to me that my friend Adam Brown had been killed by enemy fire during an op. Adam and I had been together for years going back to Team Two. We'd gone through S&T together; we'd deployed together. I had dressed Adam's hand after the Humvee accident, and we'd endured SERE school side by side in our plywood boxes. Adam had been a great man, a real warrior. It was a tough loss, made tougher by the fact that Adam had a wife and two young children. In our own impromptu memorial, I opened a bottle of liquor and my team leader did the same. We took shots over the phone and began telling our favorite Adam stories.

Heading to a target with a warrior who never quit, Adam Brown. Fearless.

※ ※ ※

When my squadron returned from Afghanistan, I had to get back to doing at least some work. I arranged for a babysitter from the neighborhood to watch Triston when I needed to go to the compound to practice picking locks or some other breacher task.

My days at work grew longer as I eased my way back into Team life. I also began taking French language classes to expand my knowledge base. With the guys back from Afghanistan, I was able to train with them a bit more, as well. If they were doing something locally, I did my best to be there. I shot with them and jumped in on training missions wherever I could to help. It was usually only a few hours a day, but it got me out of the house. I was back as part of the team, and I felt like I was doing something productive. No one gave me a hard time about the part-time role that I was playing; everyone understood and appreciated my predicament.

My situation was unusual, but not unique. A few months into my job as a full-time parent, my old instructor Ollie, who had pleaded with me to join his squadron, was himself awarded sole custody of his kids. He had mentored me on my journey to become an assaulter, and now I helped him learn about fatherhood. Soon after that, two more great operators got their kids, as well. Every year on the second Sunday in May, I send each of them a text wishing them a "Happy Mother's Day."

By becoming a single father, the career that I had worked so hard to build suddenly became uncertain. I couldn't exactly leave the kids at home with babysitters while I deployed overseas, but if I couldn't deploy, I wasn't doing my job. At some point, my superiors would have to decide what to do with me—they couldn't hide me forever. And I wasn't sure how I would even make a living and support my family if I couldn't be with the SEAL Team.

A glimpse into the chaos that was single fatherhood. In hindsight, we had a lot of fun.

※　※　※

My teammate Jason Workman and I were at a lock-picking course in Tulsa, Oklahoma. We took a lunch break one day at a local restaurant with one of the instructors and his wife. Jason and I had been breaking into cars all day and were dressed about like construction workers. At some point we had to use the bathroom at the same time so, like a couple of girlfriends, we grabbed our purses and went. On the way, we walked by a table with two very attractive women sitting at it, and gave one another a look.

Jason and I hadn't quite finished our conversation about them before we sat back down, and something piqued our instructor's wife's curiosity. "What are you guys talking about?" she asked. "We just saw two chicks," I said. Five minutes later, she went to the restroom and struck up a conversation with the two young women on the way. She invited them to come out with us that night and they accepted.

Anna was tall, with an athletic build and dirty blond hair. A mortgage broker, she was tough as nails; we hit it off instantly and had a fun night together. She gave Jason and me a ride home and, when we were sitting in the parking lot to say goodnight, I asked her if she wanted to come up to my room with me. She hesitated, as anyone would with a relative stranger, and I was sure that she was going to pass. But ever the team player, Jason reached up from the backseat and snatched the keys out of the ignition. He got out of the car and started walking toward the hotel. "Now you *have* to come up," he said. She did—and by the time I left Tulsa, I'd stumbled into a long-distance relationship.

▪   ▪   ▪

Our divorce was finalized, and things more or less stabilized between Leia and me. She seemed to be in a better place mentally and emotionally under her parents' roof.

Our court-ordered custody agreement was for her to have the kids every other weekend; beyond the regular visits, she was entitled to two weeks uninterrupted time with the children during the summer. With her living in Memphis, an every-other-weekend arrangement wasn't going to be feasible, either logically or financially.

Regardless of how I felt about her, my kids needed to have a relationship with their mother. I made the decision that, since she wasn't seeing them every other week, she could have the entire summer with them. Her parents are good people and I knew that they would look out for the kids' well-being.

There was a side benefit to me if the kids could be away on that schedule. Call it fear of the unknown and a need for closure, or a desire to stay in the fight and gain pure revenge—Adam's death meant that I had to get back on a deployment. It just so happened that the timing of my squadron's next trip to Afghanistan aligned perfectly with my kids' summer break. I asked permission to jump in, and the request was approved.

Jason urged me to deploy along with his troop, which my other close friend Matt "Milsy" Mills was also a part of. Though Jason, Millsy, and I were close buddies, we had never worked side by side while overseas. I had lobbied hard to get Jason assigned with me when he joined our SEAL Team, but the team didn't need two breachers, so he was assigned to a different troop, where Millsy was. We deployed at the same time but often found ourselves billeted at different bases. Sometimes my troop would work with theirs on operations, but other times it didn't, so I wasn't seeing those guys on a daily basis. By joining them, I would also become part of Adam Brown's troop, alongside the guys who had been with him during his last moments on this earth.

Though it was incredibly tempting to head downrange with Jason, I was loyal to my own team first. I decided that, if I was going back to war, it would be with my boys. It was a tough decision, at the time. Little did I know that it would save my life.

※　※　※

A week or so before my deployment, my ex-wife's parents drove from Memphis to pick up the kids, and I met them outside. I'd always liked and respected her father and happily shook his hand. Her mother tried to give me a hug but, given the way that she'd reacted when I got custody of the kids, I wasn't having it.

As I watched my children, who I'd been solely responsible for, drive away, I exhaled deeply and felt the weight of the world lifted off my shoulders—it was the greatest relief of my life. But by an hour later, the quiet in the house was deafening. I missed them already. I'd grown accustomed to the chaos of having a family.

I did my best to push aside the feeling in my gut and focus on the mission. It was time to get back into the fight.

I ran into Jason at the Command just before we each flew overseas and, as usual, I told him to be careful.

Saying goodbye to my kids before my final deployment.
Kailha, Samantha, and Triston—you saved my life. Thank you.

HOT WASH

Up until just a few years ago, my life was a never-ending cycle of work/fail, work/fail, work/fail. It took me nearly a decade to sit back and really appreciate what I have.

I didn't realize it in the heat of the moment, but gaining custody of my kids was the defining positive moment in my life. Getting to know each of them and learning how to be their father was better than getting my Trident, earning my squadron patches, or fighting overseas with my buddies. What I thought was the end for me turned out to be the beginning. **My kids taught me so much about life and about myself.** I know that I made mistakes, but I also know that I did my best and wouldn't change anything for the world.

There's no question that this was also one of the most stressful times of my life. What ultimately got me through it was something that I learned in the military. **When you have multiple tasks to perform, you prioritize them and execute accordingly.** When I have five bad guys in front of me, I don't worry about all of them—I worry about the one who is the greatest threat. Focus on the ten-meter target before you worry about the one at fifty.

That said, life is not the military. Barking orders at your family is not the answer. I had to learn to shift my tone to one that was more appropriate. Know your audience.

NIGHT OF KNIGHTS

✝

t was the summer of 2011 and I was back where I belonged. Back with my boys, going after bad guys night after night; business as usual. It felt good to be in the action again after missing my squadron's previous deployment. The selfish part of me felt great being there. Every time we took out an insurgent, it felt like an incremental step toward avenging Adam's death. It was different this time though, after spending so much time with my kids. For the first time, I really felt like I was missing something by being away. Rationally though, even if I were home in Virginia Beach, they would be with their mother all summer and I wouldn't see them anyway.

There was a noticeable change in my risk tolerance on this deployment, no doubt thanks to my newfound role as a parent.

My life meant more to me. While before I was fine with dying if that's what fate decided, I now felt responsible for those kids. The thought of them spending the rest of their lives with their mother made me a more careful and deliberate warrior. In hindsight, I treated my own life on that deployment the way that I should have done all along.

On my first op, I turned a corner and nearly stumbled over a dead insurgent that one of our snipers had taken out. He was wearing manjammies and had multiple RPG rockets concealed underneath. His body had collapsed in an awkward position on the ground with the rockets poking upward like poles on a circus tent. The cloth draped over the rockets gave him a very distorted look. Through night vision, I couldn't make sense of what was where in terms of his anatomy. Knowing that he had explosives strapped to his body, I couldn't simply pass him by without ensuring that he was down for good.

The last time I'd shot a bad guy with ordnance strapped to him I'd gotten shrapnel in my eye socket and a Purple Heart medal for my troubles. Setting off one of the rockets would have killed or wounded me and at least two of my teammates. The old Eddie would have just fired at whatever body part was exposed to see if he moved, but this time I hesitated for just a moment, trying to decide what to do. What was probably five seconds felt like an eternity. It was so unlike me that my teammate asked me about it after the fact. He knew I'd taken on responsibility for my kids and he wanted to make sure my head was still in the game. "You good, man?" I was.

While I had become more cautious, I was still addicted to the action. When we got back to our base, the intel guys showed me a drone video of twenty to thirty armed insurgents running out of a building to escape us that evening. On the video feed, they looked like ants pouring out of the structure. Less than a minute before their escape, I had been standing by that very same door. A normal human would have been relieved to have avoided facing so many armed men but, instead, I was furious. Despite only having twenty-eight rounds in my rifle's magazine, I would have loved the chance at so many kills. And people wonder why guys like me have trouble adapting back into society.

Later in that deployment we went on one of the toughest operations of my career. Our mountain infil was so strenuous that guys were getting IVs to rehydrate before we hit the target. By then I was in my thirties, and the relentless pace of the job had taken its toll on my body. My knees, back, and shoulders were shot, but I pressed on. Between my physical condition and the value that I'd placed on my life, I knew in my heart that this would be my final deployment.

The trip flew by, and before I knew it I only had a few days left until I would head back to the States.

One night, my troop was supposed to go out, but there was bad weather and, as I remember it, our birds from the 160th weren't able to operate. Our sister troop, Jason's unit, was located at a different base that had better flying conditions, and was to go out that night to support a detachment of Army Rangers who were trying to capture a senior Taliban leader. Instead of the usual birds, they would be aboard conventional CH-47D Chinooks piloted by soldiers from the Army National Guard.

With no mission, we were lounging around, watching a movie, while the other troop worked. For me, summer break was nearly over, and it was time to go back to fatherhood. With only a handful of days left, it hit me that this would probably be the last time I'd see combat.

It was just after 2 a.m. when everything changed. Our team leader ran into the room to tell us that one of the birds had gone down. We all rushed to the TOC (Tactical Operations Center), where Command and support staff were monitoring and controlling the mission. One of the large screen TVs in the room (we called it "Kill TV") had a bird's eye view of the scene, as one of the air assets beamed back video in real time.

The Rangers were on the ground taking care of the target. We knew that there were two Chinooks flying above the area; all of our boys would be together on one aircraft, the one with the callsign Extortion 17. We hoped and prayed that the bird that went down was the empty one. Losing the aircrew on the empty bird would be tragic, but the alternative would be catastrophic. I waited impatiently, my eyes fixed on the screen, as the thermal camera worked its way to the crash site. When the images of the crashed aircraft entered the screen, my heart sank: Extortion 17 was demolished and engulfed in flames.

Time slowed to a crawl and everything became blurry. I was in shock. I could see three to five twisted bodies, which had spilled off the Chinook's rear ramp during the crash, lying on the ground. We always sat in the same spot on the helicopters; Jason and Millsy sat at the very rear, just as I did. I knew that what I was seeing were the bodies of two of my closest friends: SEALs, fathers, and husbands. As I watched, their white-hot thermal signatures faded to black as the life drained from them. I can only describe it as surreal.

There was no time to mourn their deaths: it was time to go help. Everywhere you looked, guys were putting their kit on, strapping on helmets and body armor, loading weapons. We were optimistic that at least some of our boys were still alive and needed boots on the ground. We prepared ourselves for a rescue operation and began grabbing kit we might need, such as quickie saws to cut open the aircraft.

Our commanding officer told us in no uncertain terms to stand down: we weren't going out; the Rangers would handle the rescue and recovery operations. We were pissed. I personally was so angry that I was bordering on blatant insubordination. These were our guys, and it was our duty to get out there and handle whatever the situation was. In hindsight, though, he was right. We were running on emotion, and he was thinking rationally. He didn't want the charred and mutilated remains of our comrades to be our last images of them.

No one slept as we awaited word from the ground. The Rangers arrived at the crash site after 4 a.m. and found no survivors. There were thirty-eight men aboard Extortion 17, and all of them had been killed, more or less instantly, when an RPG impacted the bird's rotor, causing the bird to crash. Some illiterate insurgent wearing sandals had fired a cheap Soviet rocket and gotten lucky. That crude weapon took down a sophisticated aircraft loaded with America's best and brightest. There were fifteen members of our SEAL Unit on that bird, augmented by two other SEALs and five NSW support personnel. Three Air Force special operators were also aboard, along with the five Army flight crew members and a military working dog. Seven Afghan commandos died, as well as one interpreter. Overall, thirty-one Americans and seven allied troops died that night on a remote hillside in the Tangi Valley. It was the worst disaster in US special operations history and the greatest loss of US and allied personnel in a single event in the two-decades-long war in Afghanistan.

Years later, I spoke to one of the Rangers who led the recovery operation; though he didn't know any of the men who'd died, what he saw that morning changed his life. He even got a tattoo honoring their memory. I've always appreciated the fact that, regardless of branch of service, we share the same red, white, and blue American flag on our kit. We are one team.

Over a decade has passed since then; there's been a great deal of Monday morning quarterbacking, and numerous conspiracy theories have arisen surrounding the Extortion 17 disaster. I don't have all of the answers, but my position is simple: it doesn't matter. Bad things happen in war and, tragically, those men are gone; no amount of hand wringing or blame can bring them back. I respect the grief of the families and their search for answers, but I prefer to honor the memory of those close to me by talking about the way they lived, rather than how they died.

Stateside, members of the Command began the sad process of informing the men's surviving loved ones that they wouldn't be coming home. These were the knocks on the door dreaded by every mother, father, spouse, or sibling of a member of our armed forces.

Jason's wife, Stacey, was devastated but showed her characteristic strength and grace. She asked that I escort his remains back to his native Utah, and I accepted without hesitation. Many of the bodies were unidentifiable, at least with the technology that was available overseas; our Unit's doctor had helped identify as many individuals as possible, using tattoos and other visible physical features. When the time came, I asked him to show me the way to Jason's aluminum casket as it was being loaded onto a C-17 transport aircraft that would be taking the boys home to their families. There were so many bodies that it took two C-17s to carry them all. Some of the remains, still unidentified, were separated from the bodies; there were extra caskets filled with nothing but body parts.

The Air Force crews showed tremendous respect for the fallen men and even hung the American flag and our squadron flag from the rafters of the aircraft. There was a solemn and moving ceremony as the bodies were loaded onto the C-17. When I think about hearing the national anthem that day on the tarmac as thirty-one great men began their final journey home, I swell with pride. **This is why we stand when it is played!**

You travel relatively light when going back and forth to the States, because most of your gear is locked in containers. I had some sleeping gear in my pack, and I made a nest for myself alongside Jason's casket, which was strapped to the aircraft's metal floor. There is a nowfamous photo of a SEAL's loyal Labrador retriever lying beside his casket, refusing to leave his side. That was me, curled up alongside my best friend. I would not leave Jason unless I had to use the bathroom. I slept there, albeit not well, and I ate there. I played his favorite songs on my headphones and thought about all of the great times that we'd had together—the days spent watching *Wedding Crashers* overseas, the nights spent lifting weights, and hanging out with our families during backyard barbecues. Even with his body lying only inches away, I couldn't believe that he was gone.

I thought about the mark Jason had left on me and on the world around him. He was a good-hearted man who had shown me how good people could be. From the first day that I met him at Fort A.P. Hill, I'd felt his positive energy. When I was at the height of my selfishness, he had taught me how to be a mentor. His thirst for knowledge had made me a better SEAL, a better leader, and a better man.

By the time that we landed at the Air Force Base in Dover, Delaware, where all fallen servicemen are received, most of the families who were able to travel there had arrived. As we taxied toward the massive hangar where the remains would be unloaded, I could see dozens of people standing on the tarmac. Stacey was there, holding their son, Jax, alongside Jason's parents and brothers.

We shuffled down the ramp and into a building where the families were waiting. Those of us who had escorted the bodies had been up for three days; we were all zombies. I was on-edge.

President Obama came out to meet the family members and pay his respects to the men as their commander-in-chief. The special operations community is pretty conservative, politically. I didn't vote for him and I disagree with many of his policies, but I'll have to say that he earned my respect that day. As we gathered in a meeting area before the ceremony, he greeted every single family member—wife, parent, child—and service member in attendance. Still clad in our MultiCam-patterned cammies, we hugged our squadron mates' families, said what few words we could muster, and then began the process of offloading the remains.

As the flag-draped caskets were carried off, we all gathered and watched. It was a stifling August day, and the president stood in the hangar in a business suit at rigid attention, his right hand held in a crisp hand salute for the more than forty-five minutes that it took to unload the caskets. There were no TV cameras. By showing his respect to those men, he earned ours.

Meeting President Obama at Dover Air Force Base after flying home with my fallen brothers who perished on Extortion 17.

While the bodies were being processed by the professionals who handle the grim task, I had time to fly home and grab some belongings. It was the first time that I had left my friend's side in days. My girlfriend Anna flew in from Tulsa and met me in Virginia Beach, where we spent one night together.

Then I gathered some clothes along with my dress blues, and made my way back to Dover for the trip to Jason's hometown of Blanding, Utah. His body was loaded onto a small "Angel Flight"

jet alongside that of a soldier who had died in a separate operation. Besides the crew, it was just an Army escort and me on the
plane. Neither of us was in a mood to talk. We stopped in St. Louis,
the soldier's final resting place, before continuing on to the rocky
desert of southern Utah.

At the funeral home, it was my job to recover the folded American
flag from inside Jason's casket and make sure everything was in
order. I opened the lid and saw that the team in Dover had wrapped
his body tightly in a green wool blanket. Call it closure, but I had to
touch him. I could tell right away that he was much shorter than his
six-foot, two-inch height. As I ran my hands down the fabric that
covered his body, I found out why: parts of his legs were missing.

The logistics of burying so many men from a single unit must
have been enormous. Funerals were scattered across the nation,
and the Command chartered a bus to transport our teammates
from town to town. It took the procession more than two weeks to
make its way west to Utah. Because I was with Jason, I wasn't able
to attend any of the other services.

Jason had been a huge music fan, and Robert Earl Keen was his
favorite artist. One of our fellow teammates got in touch with Keen
and told him Jason's story. He made the trip to Blanding in time for
Jason's service and, during the ceremony, sat alone at the altar with
his guitar, standing to play his song "I'm Coming Home" in front of a
silent audience. No one clapped, but we were all moved by the music
and his generosity. When the song was over, he quietly returned to
his seat. Jason would have been blown away by this gesture.

That night, family members, teammates, and high school friends
all gathered to have a few drinks and celebrate Jason's memory.
We headed out to the desert, where we gathered at Jason's favorite

camping spot. A giant overhead outcropping of red stone made for a natural amphitheater called Spirit Cave, where we built a huge bonfire. It was the kind of place where people had no doubt gathered for centuries. It was a fitting tribute.

Though the memorial services took place in hometowns across the US, Jason and twelve other men were to be buried alongside one another at Arlington National Cemetery. Some had chosen to be buried in their hometowns, but my buddies Jason and Millsy, along with several others, wanted to be in Arlington. I made the trip back to Virginia with him, staying by his side until he reached his final resting place. Most of the members of Extortion 17 were interred in that hallowed ground, together for eternity.

It was a dreary, overcast day in northern Virginia. I stood behind Stacey and looked at Jason's son, Jax, along with all of the other children of the fallen men. The older kids knew what was happening, but many of the younger ones did not, and would probably have no memory of their fathers. It was heartbreaking. Jax was the same age as Triston, and I'd known him since he was born. I knew in that moment that I would never go to war again—I could not risk putting my own children in this situation.

Stacey and Jason had a thing for rainbows. She was always pointing them out to him; it was part of their identity. As the service was about to begin, the most crisp and beautiful rainbow that I'd ever seen arched across the sky behind us. Stacey turned to me and said, "Look, a rainbow." It was as if Jason was sending us a message that he was okay. I had maintained my composure until then, but then I lost it.

An officer presented Stacey with a folded American flag, which she accepted stoically. F/A18s flew over in the classic missing man formation, and an honor guard fired a salute. A lone bugler played "Taps." Like the other SEALs in attendance, I marched forward and stood by Jason once more. Following our tradition, I pulled the golden Trident badge from my chest and pressed it into the veneer of the casket. I did the same for Millsy, that Viking Berserker who epitomized the fearless American warrior.

A simple granite marker at Section 60 of Arlington National Cemetery reads:

EXTORTION 17

AUGUST 6, 2011

AFGHANISTAN

HERE LIE THE

MEN OF

EXTORTION 17

BELOVED

FATHERS

HUSBANDS

BROTHERS

AND SONS

"Greater love hath no man than this, that a man lay down his life for his friends."

—John 15:13

HOT WASH

Watching those bodies being unloaded from the helicopter when they arrived from the crash site made me realize how quickly everything can be taken from us. Cherish your time with family and friends, do what you love to do, and pursue your passion and purpose, because you never know when your story will end. In many parts of the world, life is cheap, and people are expendable.

Seeing the wives, children, brothers, sisters, mothers, and fathers of those men when we arrived at Dover was heartbreaking. Each individual makes their mark on the world and on their family; do your best to make your legacy positive. Avoid the materialistic trappings of society and work every day to make someone's life better. No one cared what kind of car those men drove, how many followers they had, or how much was in their bank account: what is remembered is how they lived their lives. **Live a life worth remembering**. Without ever knowing it, Jason taught me that lesson.

A WARRIOR'S REALITY

After Extortion 17, I was devastated. The loss of so many lives had a profound effect on the Command, as well as on all of us as individuals. Given the length of the pipeline and the timeline for putting operators into teams, it would take years to catch up after losing so many lives, with their cumulative experience. You can't just flip a switch to bring that many seasoned operators into the fold.

It all just seemed like a bad dream, but every morning I would wake up and realize once again that it was real. Sometimes I would get distracted and would forget for a moment, but then I'd have the urge to call or text Jason or Millsy about something, and the pain would return. Being back home with my kids helped, at least temporarily. By staying busy, I could suppress what I was feeling and drive forward. That's what a man is supposed to do, right?

I poured all of my energy into my family and work. I would wake up early, make lunches, feed the kids breakfast, and get everyone to school. Triston would head to daycare for a few hours while I went into work. Once again, my leaders were fantastic: they kept things as flexible as possible for me and allowed me to stay at the Command in what was primarily a training role.

I spent my days working in a breacher training cell. One of the things that I did during that time was develop a database of how to defeat every brand and type of lock that we could locate. The idea was that an operator on a mission could look at a lock, consult the electronic database, and immediately know what the best tool and technique for the job was.

I enjoyed it, but it wasn't like being on a team; I missed the boys. Now and then I would show up in the team room; but I always felt awkward there. Everyone treated me well; I just knew that I no longer belonged. I'm not sure if they saw it this way, but from my perspective, I was an outsider. I was out of the operational loop and wasn't contributing anything to them. It was a lonely and deeply unfamiliar feeling.

When I wasn't picking or breaking locks, I was instructing others in the art and science of explosive breaching. Part of this job was supervising various groups as a range safety officer to ensure that no one got hurt. We trained a number of police SWAT teams, and many days, I would watch carefully as they learned to blow open doors. Though they were using very small charges, each blast would leave me with the most intense headaches that I'd ever felt. After several hundred explosive breaches over the years, I had grown sensitive to the concussions. We now know a great deal about the cumulative effects of traumatic brain injuries, but it wasn't something that we paid much attention to back then. The reality is that, just like a football player or a boxer, my brain had been pummeled by explosive overpressure for years and had suffered damage.

I noticed another thing during this period also: a change in my temper. After that last deployment, the slightest thing would set me off into a rage. I'd find myself yelling at the television after a bad call during a football game; something on the news could set me off. I'd find myself chewing out strangers in the gym for not putting their weights back on the rack, or yelling at guys at the Command for minor mistakes. Some of that anger was directed at my kids. I didn't like it, but I couldn't figure out how to control it.

Jumping out of airplanes and helicopters and smashing down doors for a living takes a toll on the rest of body, too. I was a mess physically, and multiple operations were required to relieve some of the pain and allow me some reasonable mobility. Both of my shoulders were operated on, along with two surgeries on the same knee, and I had multiple hernias repaired. My right foot was damaged from mule-kicking so many doors and needed work as well.

No one likes surgery, but I learned that I loved the way the post-surgical opioid painkillers made me feel. They took away any feeling, any pain—they numbed my body, but also my emotions. They were happiness in a bottle. I would take all of them, whether I needed them or not. I would sit on the couch, telling my kids how much I loved them and feeling content for the first time in ages. When the pills ran out, and they always did, so did my happiness.

I also took cold medicine, which gave me extremely vivid dreams. Most of them involved me killing bad guys. The only action that I was seeing was in my sleep but, still, I thrived on it. The dreams weren't always ones where the good guys won. My buddies died over and over, night upon night.

When Luis died in Iraq, I had taken some solace in the fact that my last words to him had been "I love you." With Jason, there was no such comfort; I never got the chance to say goodbye to him before that terrible night. I can vividly remember a dream in which I watched as a group from my squadron was boarding an aircraft to go out on a jump. I saw a figure that I knew was Jason by his silhouette, though I couldn't see his face. He stepped out of rank toward me and I walked up to meet him. In my dream, I gave him a fist bump. As soon as our hands touched, I bolted awake. I could physically feel our hands touching as I regained consciousness. I know now that it was Jason, saying goodbye.

Though some of my physical injuries were being addressed by the Navy, no one thought to pay any serious attention to my, and our, mental health. Sure, there were mandatory visits to the shrink after each deployment, but it was just checking a box. During one of these visits, the doctor asked me what I thought about when I went to a movie theater. I told him how I would select my seat based on the layout of the room and any doorways, to put myself in the best position to defend myself. He acted like I was nuts. "What do you think is going to happen?" he said, "it's a movie theater. You're paranoid." Months later, some nutjob in Aurora, Colorado, killed a dozen people and injured fifty-eight more when he opened fire on a crowded theater. On my next mandatory visit, I went and found that doctor. "Who's crazy now, asshole?"

That doctor, like many who have never experienced the harsh realities of war and terrorism, was living with his head in the sand.

I've seen what humans are capable of and can never turn off the part of my brain that works to protect myself and my family. The reality is that no one ever walks out their door and says, "I'm going to be a victim today." Violence just happens, and when it does, you need to be ready for it. Little things like choosing the right seat in a restaurant can make the difference between life and death. Call me paranoid if you'd like; I call it vigilant.

The booze began to take hold of me again as well during this period in my life. One bottle of wine at night would turn into two. I wasn't getting crazy, but quietly drinking myself into a stupor to suppress the pain. I was exhibiting some of the exact behaviors that I'd long criticized Leia for. I kept everyone fed and clothed, but I was zoned out most of the time. To say that I was emotionally detached would be an understatement. My sleep suffered, and I noticed that even my beloved workouts had gone downhill. It wasn't merely the loss of my friends that was taking its toll. I missed being out working with the boys; I missed having a purpose. I needed a change, or it wasn't going to end well.

Virginia Beach became a place full of bad memories for me. Like remaining in a house where some tragedy occurred, I had near-constant reminders of the loss I'd suffered. It seemed like every time we went to a restaurant, memories of being there with my buddies would flash into my head. I would be in a store and run into a widow from the squadron, or pull into a gas station and then remember that Jason and I had joked around wrestling in that parking lot. It was constant. Seeing the kids without a father was always the toughest. I realized that I needed a clean slate: to be in a community where I had no memories and could start over.

I had a couple of years left before I could retire, so I began to look at other career options within the Navy. I discovered that a recruiting coordinator position was vacant. A recruiting coordinator works with local recruiters to identify potential candidates for special warfare roles (SEALs, EOD, SWCC, AIRR, and Navy diver), commit them to an enlistment, and then prepare them for their training. It was a very flexible job, ideal for a single father.

A position was open in Houston, but it wasn't the location that I wanted (Anna was still in Tulsa) so I passed on it. We maintained our long-distance relationship for another two years until the position that I was waiting for opened up, with a territory that encompassed both north Texas and all of Oklahoma. Eventually Anna became my fiancé, and this new job could bring us together under the same roof. As much as I hated to move my kids yet again, I believed it was the right choice for our family.

My orders came fast. Even though I'd long decided that Virginia Beach wasn't the place for me, it was still tough leaving the Command. I'd worked most of my life to become a part of something special, and now I was walking away from it permanently. I'd spent twelve long years in the Teams, six of which were at an elite SEAL Unit. Becoming a single father and losing so many close friends had changed everything, though, and it was time to go.

There were no parties, no ceremony, nothing to commemorate closing this chapter on my life. Being in the Teams is like being on a train: when it's time for someone to step off, the train has to keep moving. My squadron had already pushed out for a real-world mission a few days before I separated, which meant that there was no one around to see before I left. One day I simply walked off the compound and never returned.

HOT WASH

Being at the Command was a lesson in what great leadership means. When I had to step up and take responsibility for my family, my leaders had my back. After the devastation of Extortion 17, those same leaders put me into a training role so that I could continue to support my family. **In life and in your career, seek out a supportive environment that values you as the individual.** When you are in a leadership position, be empathetic to those on your team. When life throws a team member an unexpected curve, give that person the space and support to deal with it appropriately. One day, someone might return the favor.

Point of view is everything. Instead of being depressed by so many memories in Virginia Beach, I should have appreciated the good times I'd had there. **You can't always change your situation, but you can always change your attitude.** Carry the good memories forward and leave the pain of the past in the past.

Walking away from my dream job was tough, but it was the right thing to do. **Know when to walk away.** After John Elway and the Denver Broncos won the Super Bowl in 1999, he could have stuck around for another season. Instead, he chose to go out on top. I'm sure he hadn't lost the competitive fire that had made him a champion, but he knew that it was his time to go.

You can dwell on the past or focus on the future. Though I missed the Teams, I knew that my time there was done. By getting my degree and beginning to map out what my life would look like post-military, I chose the future.

Doors will close and new doors will open. Walk through them and own the room.

LOST AND FOUND

When I arrived in Dallas to check in for my new job, I was hit head-on by the reality of the conventional military. Though I'd been told multiple times that I could live anywhere within my area of responsibility, that wasn't the case when I actually showed up for work. The master chief in charge told me in no uncertain terms that I had to live in Dallas.

The whole point of me taking this job was to give me a support system; I didn't know anyone in Dallas and certainly wasn't going to ask Anna to move there. This was the same attitude that I'd encountered in the Marines, and, after so much time in special warfare, I wasn't going to put up with it. I got a little aggressive with the master chief and told him flat out that I wasn't moving to Dallas. I promised that I would get the job done no matter what, but that I had to be in Tulsa. He wasn't used to being spoken to that way, and it took him by surprise. I don't know if it was the Trident on my chest, my size, or the look on my face, but, after a few tense moments, he relented.

The kids and I arrived in Tulsa and I rented a house near Anna. After the way my first marriage had ended, I wasn't ready to commit to moving my family in with her just yet. This was definitely a joint decision. She had two daughters around the same ages as Kailha and Sammie, and everyone got along well. Having a fiancé and four older girls to help with Triston was a real blessing that allowed me to get on the road and do my job.

I would give speeches at high schools, sit down with potential candidates, and even hold two or three workouts a week to prepare the interested young men and women for what was ahead of them. To my surprise, several of the candidates couldn't take the physical and mental stress of the workouts I was leading them through. Some of these kids were driven to tears. I sat them down and did my best to talk them out of this pipeline, knowing that they would never make it.

I was expected to deliver a certain number of candidates per month to feed the everincreasing demand for special warfare operators. I quickly learned that the quotas set out by the recruiting command were unrealistic. If an individual is not 100 percent committed to becoming a special operator, it's never going to happen. There's a reason that BUD/S and other training programs have such high dropout rates: they're not for everyone. I wasn't going to force these kids into failure if their hearts weren't in it. I did my best to put into the pipeline only those young men and women who I felt had a real chance of making it. If I was no longer going to be on a Team, I could at least make sure that the Teams had the best candidates that I could find.

I bounced back and forth between Tulsa, Oklahoma City, and Dallas, meeting with candidates, testing them physically, and coordinating with the talent scouts under me. I was on the road plenty but, compared to being at the Command, my time away from home was minimal.

We settled into our own little Brady Bunch version of normalcy and, as always, my kids adapted well to our new surroundings. My kiddos are studs. But in hindsight, I was just going through the motions as a father. I really wasn't there for them in a meaningful way.

With three years left until I could retire, I began preparing for my post-military future. I may not have been emotionally available for my kids, but I certainly wanted to take care of them. In the military, you are more or less taken care of; you never have to wonder whether your next paycheck will come. It was stressful knowing that this train would end when I retired and that I would need to provide for my family in a new, less stable environment.

I was great at my job, but there was virtually no carryover to the civilian world. I wasn't sure exactly what I wanted to do when I retired, but the one thing I *was* certain of was that I didn't want to work for someone else.

If I was going to be my own boss, I needed to expand my knowledge base beyond breaching and CQB. It was time to take advantage of the military's 100 percent tuition assistance program. I had taken some college courses as a Marine, and I continued my education by taking classes online. Before long, I earned a bachelor's degree in security management. (Yes, that's a real thing. Who knew?)

On the surface, everything was going well but, in reality, this move hadn't been the perfect change of scene that I'd idealized back in Virginia Beach. I missed the Teams, I missed being with the guys, and I missed the action. Though I still wore a Trident on my uniform, I was effectively no longer a deployable SEAL. Dealing with the conventional Navy mentality of the recruiters didn't help. I had no friends in Oklahoma, and my friends who were still alive were busy taking the fight to the bad guys. It was a very dark and lonely time in my life.

Beyond being bored and relatively unhappy at work, my emotional wounds ran deep. I put a bandage over them, but they festered underneath. I thought constantly about the friends that I'd lost and all of the lives that I'd taken. I'm proud of every shot that I fired in defense of this country, but even killing evil men can take its toll, and it took out of me more than my share. I wouldn't change a thing, but there's no doubt that what I'd seen and done had diminished my ability to have actual feelings.

My friend and fellow retired SEAL Mike Ritland calls this the "narrowing of the emotional bandwidth," which I believe describes it well. If I had any real feelings, I continued to find ways to suppress them. My drinking hadn't slowed down, either. I was still acting like I was hanging out with my hard-partying teammates. Anna wasn't amused, and cracks in our relationship began to emerge.

Things came to a head one night when I accompanied her on a night out with her coworkers, who included her brother. He'd rented a party bus to take us out for a night on the town in the booming metropolis of Oklahoma City. I hadn't been out partying in some time, and I was a little too enthusiastic about making sure that I properly enjoyed myself. I started hitting the Captain

Morgan rum-and-Cokes pretty hard at 5 p.m. and didn't slow down. I blacked out at some point in the night but, unfortunately, that wasn't the end of the story. Somehow, one of Anna's coworkers decided that it was a good idea to climb on top of me and give me a lap dance. I apparently shared her enthusiasm. I did not keep my hands to myself and, justifiably, Anna got upset. Her reaction set me off and, in a fit of rage, I told her that I was going to "cut off her fucking face." Classy, right?

For the record, I had no intention of laying a hand on her. I'd spent a decade in a world where people said, and sometimes did, things like that on a daily basis, but I had not adjusted to the civilian world, where such threats of violence were unacceptable. I woke up at Anna's the next morning with my head pounding. As soon as I saw Anna's face, I knew that something bad had happened.

Anna drove me home and sat next to me on the couch, asking whether I remembered what I'd said and done the night before. I had no idea, but the fact that we were having this conversation meant that it was nothing good. She gave me a play-by-play of my drunken performance and threats of violence. I was 100 percent in the wrong, and I knew it; the problem was that I didn't know how to turn that part of me off. I sat sheepishly and stared at the floor like I was a nine-year-old in the principal's office. It was clear that she had a lot to say, and I didn't dare interrupt. At the end of her monologue, she took off her engagement ring and threw it at me, storming out of my house. *There goes that.*

A few days passed and she cooled off a bit. We ended up talking again, and this time she told me flat out that I was broken and needed to fix myself. That I needed to find God. She asked me if I would be willing to attend a men's retreat with her brother, put on by an organization called True North Ministries out of Oklahoma City, which did a version of John Eldredge's Wild at Heart program. I didn't do any research on the group; I just agreed to go to keep her happy. The event was sold to me as a weekend of shooting, watching movies, eating, and socializing. It was more or less an ultimatum anyway and, besides, how bad could hanging out with a bunch of guys for the weekend be?

I didn't really realize it at the time, but Wild at Heart is a faith-based organization. It wasn't just a men's retreat: it was a *Christian* men's retreat. The organizers describe it as a "an honest, no-BS trek into the deep passions and desires of a man's heart, the healing of the wounds he's taken in this battle, the realm of fatherhood and sex and God and calling—life as it was meant to be lived." In hindsight it sounds like exactly what the doctor ordered, but there's more to it than that. My childhood fears of all things religion bubbled to the surface, creating resistance and doubt. Had I known what this Wild at Heart retreat was all about, I might not have agreed to go.

▪ ▪ ▪

The retreat was a couple of hours away from Tulsa, and I made the drive on a leisurely Thursday afternoon. I didn't give too much thought to what the weekend might bring, though the idea of hanging out with a group of guys was appealing, since I had no real friends in the area. Coming from the den of comradery that is the Teams, it was tough not having those types of connections. The unfortunate fact was that my closest friends were dead.

I drove to Oklahoma City and caught a ride the rest of the way. We pulled into a parking lot of what looked like a kids' summer camp. There was a large cabin-style building, surrounded by smaller structures, and lots of open land. It had been a long week, and I was looking forward to grabbing a glass of red wine. I followed the signs into an auditorium where guys were setting up folding chairs in preparation for the weekend's kick-off session.

I looked around the room for something to drink. Surely there was a bar, or even just a cooler full of beer somewhere, right? Well, it turns out that you don't go to a Christian retreat to drink. This was my first sign that this weekend would be vastly different from anything that I was accustomed to, or expecting.

There were more than a hundred men in attendance, ranging in age from seventeen to seventy. Via video, John Eldredge, Wild at Heart's founder, took the stage and welcomed all of us to the retreat. His words were powerful and thought provoking, and, before long, some of the attendees began to break down into tears. Coming from a world where it was taboo to show any emotion, I was shocked. Weren't these guys embarrassed to break down in public? I didn't know what to think. The presentation was good but, in all honesty, I rolled my eyes at some of the things I was seeing and hearing. The messages were incompatible with my mindset, and I had to continually remind myself that I needed to keep an open mind.

The presenters spoke about things like "father wounds," concepts that were completely foreign to me. I didn't believe any of this stuff actually existed. My dad was a great guy, how could he have wounded me?

What they meant was that, when your father says something to you, it makes a mark on your soul. As a man, there is no more important influence than your father—whether you know it or not, he is the one you're trying to emulate and working to impress all your life. My dad's "get it done" attitude influenced me deeply and helped me be successful in special operations. On the other hand, his drinking and extracurricular activities also shaped me.

I came away from the first session a skeptic. A few points resonated, but nothing inside of me wanted to break down into tears.

In the evenings we watched classic guy movies like *Braveheart* and *Last of the Mohicans*. John and the men from True North Ministries explained the significance of movies on our culture and ourselves. Nearly every movie can be broken down into three main themes: there is a hero, there is a villain, and there is a love story. If you don't believe me, try to think of a movie that doesn't have those three elements. We love these universal stories because of their fundamental truth. When you strip them down to the basics, movies are about finding love, pursuing good, and conquering evil. That had been my life in a nutshell. Now John was speaking my language. In the Bible, Jesus is the hero, Satan is the villain, and the love story is God's grace.

I'm a very visual learner, so this format really helped me connect with what was being said. It didn't hurt that I'd watched some of these same titles dozens of times with Jason. For a moment, he was back by my side, watching good conquer evil. I thought about the themes that I missed all of the times that I'd watched these films before. It didn't take much to associate William Wallace's brutal execution at the end of *Braveheart* with Jesus' martyrdom. Things began to click.

During the days of the retreat, there were sessions on a variety of topics. One of the topics that took me by surprise was the Christian view of pornography. For most warriors, porn is part of life overseas, when we are forced to be away from our wives and girlfriends for months or longer. I always thought of porn as a harmless outlet for my urges, something that kept me from cheating on my wife. The presenters talked about pornography as a toxic element in men's lives, one that subconsciously diminished our view of women and of intimacy. "Okay," I thought. "I just want to do the right thing so, if porn is bad, I'm done with it." I was really trying.

Each day there would be three to four sessions, followed by quiet time that allowed each of us to reflect upon what we had heard. We were encouraged to take this time to pray and record our thoughts. *I'm here*, I thought; *I may as well give this a chance.* I wanted to be alone and ventured outside with a pen and my journal, looking for the perfect spot. Before long I found a small hill with a rock outcropping, about a hundred yards away. It was early in the morning, and the sun was just beginning to rise. I sat down, zipping up my jacket to fight off the chill.

I began writing my thoughts in my journal and, after a few minutes reflecting on things, decided that this was when I would ask for help from above. I closed my eyes and, for the first time in my life, attempted to pray with real sincerity. I didn't even know how to pray—I just started talking. "God, I want to know You. I want to have the connection with You that these men have. I need help, and I don't know what to do. I want to be present for my family, to live in the moment instead of always thinking about what comes next. I need Your help, God. Fix me. Show me that You are real." I felt at ease and, right on cue, the rising sun bathed my body in warmth the same way that it had on the final day of Hell Week, so many years earlier. I didn't think much of it at the time, but looking back, it was my first tangible indication that God was real.

Throughout the weekend I heard men offering to pray for other attendees. Being the belligerent and prideful asshole that I can be, my attitude was "you don't know me, how are you going to pray for me?" It just struck me as weird. What I saw, though, was men breaking down as the secrets and fears deep down inside themselves were revealed, and finding freedom from them. Afterward, it looked as if a weight had been lifted from them; they smiled for hours. As the weekend progressed, I became envious of the peace that these men had found. I am a prideful son-of-a-bitch who would never ask for it, but I hungered for someone to pray for me.

The last night there was spent around a bonfire, where we each wrote down the toxic elements of our lives that we wanted to eliminate. My list wasn't short: killing, pride, anger, excessive drinking, pornography, and my inability to forgive. Afterward, each man stood up and shared his list with the group. As my turn approached, I found myself trembling. I'd jumped out of airplanes in the darkness, charged into rooms in hostile territory, and had killed trained terrorists at close quarters, but the idea of sharing my sins with these strangers terrified me. I took a deep breath, gathered my strength, and shared. I don't recall exactly what I said, but the gist of it was, "I've been prideful, I've relied on drinking and pills, and I want to be done with all of it." I read off my list and began to tear up as I bared my soul in front of this group of men. As soon as I was done speaking, I tossed my list into the fire.

It felt good to get those things off my chest, things that I had shared with no one before that moment. My mind buzzed as the remaining men gave their own testimony. I was relieved, as if the simple act of speaking out and tossing my mistakes into the fire had begun the process of healing. That simple act represented both the actual and symbolic first steps of finding my own personal redemption and realizing my true strength.

The campfire session ended, and the crowd filtered away in different directions. I hadn't told anyone what I did for a living, but clearly Anna's brother knew. I'm not sure how, but word began to get around and I could see the looks from the others, sizing me up. A young man in his early twenties approached me and told me what I'd said was awesome and asked how I was feeling. "I'm good, dude," I told him. He then asked if he could pray for me. I was a little taken aback. Here I was, a thirty-something SEAL combat veteran, and this kid was bold enough to walk up to me with confidence. He definitely had stones. Still, I agreed, since I'd waited for just such an offer as the weekend progressed.

The simple act of him *asking* to pray for me brought up emotions that I fought hard to bottle up. The "don't show emotion" mindset that I'd carried for years was battling the feelings I was having. I closed my eyes and bowed my head. He put his hand on my shoulder and began to pray aloud. Almost immediately, I broke down in tears. I mean really broke down: I completely lost it. It was as if his words threw the switch to open whatever had bottled up my emotions for years. I was a quivering mess, with tears streaming down my face. It all came pouring out. This stranger had touched my soul in a way that no one else had.

When he ended the prayer I began to gather myself, slowing my breathing and wiping the tears from my face. He asked me if I wanted to hang out and talk for a bit, and we made our way to a patio area. We sat and talked for several hours. He encouraged me to share my story with others. I explained that I didn't know where to begin—that I had no relationship with Christ and would feel like a hypocrite if I tried to influence someone else. Though I didn't feel that it was my time, deep down I wanted it to be. I began to accept that Christ was real and that, through this young man named Kyle Thompson (who is now host of the *Undaunted Life* podcast), he was speaking to me, reaching out a hand to a struggling soul. I went to bed that night with a feeling of peace that I hadn't felt in years. I slept without the aid of alcohol or pills and felt rejuvenated when I awoke that Sunday morning.

The final day began with a worship service, the first one that I'd participated in as an adult. Matt Redman's song "10,000 Reasons (Bless the Lord)" was blaring on the sound, and everyone was singing. I joined in, not knowing the words but enthusiastically reading from the lyrics that were being projected onto screens above. I felt *alive*. It was like someone had pressed the reset button on my soul, washing away all of the bad. I was fired up.

My head was buzzing as we began the final session of the retreat. After so much darkness in my life, I felt light. I'd been rolling my eyes just days before, but now the speakers had my rapt attention. There were books that they recommended reading, and they encouraged each of us to attend services, to join a small prayer group, and to tithe. Honestly, it was all pretty overwhelming for a guy whose only real connection to religion had been craving vanilla wafers in Sunday school. Being a Christian sounded hard. It seemed like they were asking a lot of us, and I wasn't sure that I had enough to give.

They closed the session by recognizing individuals who had stood out during the retreat, giving honorable mentions to those who had given moving testimony. Obviously I hadn't said anything profound, so I was sure that I wouldn't hear my name called. Other than my brief remarks during the campfire and a couple of side conversations, I'd more or less kept to myself all weekend. When the presenters said that they wanted to recognize the attendee who had changed the most during the retreat, I wondered who it would be. Then I heard my name. I was shocked.

My head was swimming as I walked up to the stage while everyone applauded. I was handed a pen made from an olive tree that had grown in Jerusalem, inlayed with a small steel cross. I was moved beyond words and once again broke into tears. Others may look at that pen as a simple gift from a group of men, but to me, it was a sign from God that said "I'm real." They were right; I had changed.

I shook hands with a few of the men as the retreat broke up, reflecting on how much had happened in a short few days. I'd carpooled with Anna's brother and two other guys from Oklahoma City, and we made the hour-long drive back to where I was parked. One of the passengers, who was controlling the MP3 player, chose a rap song filled with hate, angry lyrics, and profanity. I felt repulsed by what I was hearing just minutes after leaving such a positive environment. I'm no prude, but I wanted nothing to do with that kind of negativity. I tuned out the music and sent Anna a text message, letting her know how much I'd enjoyed the weekend and that I would call her as soon as I was alone.

I said goodbye to her brother and climbed into my truck. I called Anna and tried my best to convey the events of the retreat, but every time that I began to speak, I broke into tears and couldn't continue. I'm not sure how many times I had to hang up, compose myself, and call her back, but it took most of the two-hour drive to get it all out. I went straight to her house, and we sat down on the couch together. I apologized for my past behavior: the drinking, the anger, the violent outbursts. I told her that I had a lot to work on, but that I loved her and wanted to be with her.

We were both in tears and she told me that when I'd left for the retreat, she had no intention of continuing our relationship. She had been sure that she was leaving me and was never coming back. Unbeknownst to me, she had gone to St. Louis for the weekend to visit a girlfriend. Anna wasn't a party girl by any means, but she needed some fun and was ready to move on with her life. She and her friend went out to a bar, where they sat on couches, just chatting and having a good time. When a huge fight broke out, a man was knocked into her lap, spilling her drink all over her. "I should not be here," she thought. Anna left the bar and drove the six hours back to Tulsa that night. The weekend didn't go as planned for either of us, it seemed.

Days later I was still struggling to process all that had happened, still unsure about God's existence. All of the talk of being saved was great, but how could I be forgiven after all that I had done? I'd killed more men than I could count, and though I'm confident that they all deserved it, I was a killer, nonetheless. I was no Biblical scholar, but even I knew the part about "thou shall not murder." *How could I be saved?* I thought. As I asked the question, I was driving through Tulsa, passing a car wash with one of those red digital signs beckoning drivers to pull in for a scrub. Deep down, I was still skeptical of God's existence. I wanted to believe, but I just wasn't sure. *You know all of the terrible things that I've done, God; show me that You're real.* As I drove by, the sign flashed one word: SAVED.

HOT WASH

We all go through periods in our lives when we are looking for something—something to suppress the hurt, the anger. Often we look to the wrong places for salvation. We turn to sex, to alcohol, and to drugs. Those crutches only bring more pain and suffering to us and those around us. When evil forces are at work, it is the time to lean on God; He is the drug that will bring you true comfort.

Sometimes you need others to push you in the right direction. Anna did that when she not so subtly suggested that I attend the weekend retreat. Her decision, and my decision to accept that I didn't have all the answers, changed my life forever. Be that force of good that pushes people in a positive direction, not one that leads them to the darkness.

Becoming a Christian seemed overwhelming at first. View it as life's greatest opportunity. Focus on what is laid upon your heart and take things one step at a time. Once you've accepted God's grace, the rest will come easily and in due time. I'm not here to preach to you, but merely to share what changed **me** for the better.

My childhood fear of Jesus was real, but after years of reflection and prayer, I know that I had been deceived. I felt comfort and peace when he was with me, but fear set in when he disappeared. The devil held me down for thirty-two years with that deception, but the light finally broke free.

We face battles daily, so daily, prepare for war.

Stay alert! Watch out for your great enemy, the devil. He prowls around like a roaring lion, looking for someone to devour. Stand firm against him, and be strong in your faith. Remember that your family of believers all over the world is going through the same kind of suffering you are.

—I Peter 5:8–9

AM I SAVED? REALLY?

The retreat put me on a path toward a better life, but things didn't exactly improve overnight. Anna and I were back together and getting along, but I still battled my internal demons. I was going to church every Sunday, which was a positive force in my life. I would walk away feeling refreshed, and I tried to carry that feeling through the week. Still, I struggled with my newfound faith; it was a constant battle. I knew what I wanted to believe, but after a childhood fear of all things Jesus and lifetime of agnosticism, it was a process. Only later would I recognize that this was really an unseen battle between good and evil, a fight for my soul.

I did a lot of reading, trying to learn as much about the Christian faith as I could. One of the things that I learned was the power of the name of Jesus. In tough moments, I would close my eyes and speak his name under my breath, almost like a mantra. This brought me peace and comfort.

Given my background, I was particularly interested in the fight between good and evil, since I'd seen so many real-world examples of those two forces. The Christian "we love everyone" message didn't resonate too well with me. While most people are inherently good, others are not. I'd seen vile predators kill, maim, rape, and terrorize innocent civilians too many times for me to see the good in everyone. The terrorist that was casually executing innocent truck drivers tied to posts on video in Iraq didn't need me to pray for him—he needed the bullet that I gave him.

Biblical passages such as "Put on the whole armor of God, that you may be able to stand against the schemes of the devil" and "He is my loving God and my fortress, my stronghold and my deliverer, my shield, in whom I take refuge," resonated deeply with me. The Crusader patch that I'd worn proudly on my shoulder so many times in combat suddenly had new meaning to me.

I found myself looking back on moments in my life where God had revealed his presence to me: the voice that drove me to safety in the moment before Luis' death; the decision that kept me from deploying alongside Jason and the other men who died aboard Extortion 17; all of the near misses, all of the times where I knew that I would die, only to be shielded by some unseen protector. I have no doubt now who that Protector was. Roll your eyes if you want; I did the same until I sought and found peace.

God's presence in my life gave me comfort, but sometimes even that wasn't enough to win the fight raging inside of me. Every day was a struggle to avoid drinking or, if I did decide to drink, not to get blind drunk. A voice inside me would tell me *You should have died with your buddies in Afghanistan. You're never going to be able to do this. You're not a Christian, you don't know God. You're a fraud.* I was physically squirming like a junkie struggling for a fix, constantly conflicted about my life's path. *What was going to happen when I retired from the Navy? How was I going to take care of my family? What was going to happen with my relationship with Anna?* It was overwhelming.

Despite my internal struggles, Anna and I decided to move forward with our plans to marry. It was a big wedding in Tulsa, with friends and family from all over attending. Both personally and professionally, I'd come a long way from standing at the altar as a naïve teenaged Marine at my first wedding. I stood in my dress whites and, when I looked out at my friends, my family, and my children, I felt tremendous pride. It seemed like, after all of the drama, things were going to be normal. Before the wedding I'd made the decision to stop drinking, since alcohol had become such a negative force in my life. I'd had enough and decided to quit cold turkey. I went through our wedding and reception completely sober and didn't have a single drink for close to a year.

Things weren't always rosy. Marriage compounded the financial insecurity that I felt. I'd added more dependents but still didn't have a solid plan for the next phase of my life. Getting out of the military can be a strange and scary time. I'd been financially safe in the comfortable bosom of the US government since I'd graduated high school, and I was suddenly going to be on my own. Things like health insurance and retirement plans were totally unfamiliar to me. There is a reason why so many veterans struggle with this transition. I was determined that my path would be different.

Like father, like son.

In terms of my career, my saving grace came from an unusual source. Joe, my old BUD/S roommate, asked me if I wanted to do some security contracting with him overseas in my spare time. Tulsa wasn't the utopia that I'd imagined, and I was dying for something just like this. I missed the boys, missed the action, and as an enlisted sailor, I could always use some extra cash. My kids were with their mother for the summer, so there was no reason not to give it a try.

Knocking back some old-fashioneds with Joe, my BUD/S roommate.

My first foray into the civilian world of executive protection was a three-week trip to Paris to provide security for an extremely wealthy family. Our job was to prepare for every contingency and to anticipate problems long before they arose. It was much more laid-back and less visible than the executive protection work that I'd done in the military. In the civilian world, if we did things correctly, no one but the clients would even know what we were up to. That took some adjustment for someone who had spent the last several years in a hyperaggressive environment., but I adapted pretty quickly. We were there not only to physically protect the clients, but also to guard their reputations. It was engaging work and it gave me a sense of purpose and mission that my coordinator position often lacked. I can honestly say that I enjoyed it, and the money wasn't bad, either. Almost immediately, I decided that this would be my post-military niche.

The client family was pleased with my performance and, on their recommendation, I was soon accompanying other clients to film festivals in Toronto and Cannes. The French Riviera is a long way from Baghdad in terms of danger, but there were emergencies that required us to think outside of the box. It could still be stressful, but I'd seen the worst, which made things far less challenging. Still today, civil unrest is something that we are constantly on the lookout for so that we can steer our clients clear of the danger.

There was a massive struggle raging between taxi and Uber drivers in France, which led to a protest led by the French National Taxi Union. The situation had quickly escalated, and more than one hundred Uber drivers and passengers had been attacked in the weeks prior to our arrival. Things culminated with taxis effectively blockading the Nice airport in protest of their newfound competition. The protest, of course, was just in time for the Cannes Film Festival. Cannes attendees usually arrive by one of two means: yacht or private jet. We were on the ground well in advance of our clients and built a plan to get them safely transported from their aircraft to the hotel. We found what was effectively a back door out of the airfield; some palms may have been greased to allow us to use it. Whatever it takes.

There is a great deal of waiting around in the executive protection world, and the mind can wander easily. During the downtime on these contract jobs, I thought about the other skills that I had to offer. This thought process helped me develop a solid plan for life after the Navy. I could do far more than play bodyguard.

I decided to draw on my experience in executive protection, intelligence gathering, surveillance, and threat analysis to provide risk assessment and security solutions for private-sector companies and individuals. Because my mindset when planning an operation was to prepare of any contingency that might arise, I decided to name the company Contingent Solutions. The Navy, especially its special operations component, can be fairly lenient when it comes to operating one's own business while still on active duty, so I wasn't breaking any rules. It all comes down to retention; they want to keep people happy so that they will stay in the service.

Another break came when I got a call from another former operator at my old SEAL Unit. He asked whether I was still doing security and if I was interested in serving as the director of security for an international corporation. This was exactly the kind of opportunity that would make my family financially secure outside of the military. I jumped at the chance.

The company was looking to make an internal hire, but my objective was to sell them on my company, not just me. In keeping with my goal of becoming my own boss, I offered to provide them the services that they desired on a contract basis. This was my introduction to corporate America, where the wheels can sometimes turn more slowly than in the military. The selection process dragged on, involving countless phone interviews over a period of months. I felt confident that I would get the contract and was surprised and disappointed when they called to tell me that they had gone "in another direction."

I was even more surprised when, a month later, they called me back and requested that I come in for an interview. I was no less confident in my ability, but it sounded like the deck was stacked against me. My competition for the role was serious: a Marine colonel, a former CIA officer, and an Air Force intelligence specialist. Though they likely didn't have my on-the-ground experience, they were all well-educated and attractive candidates for a corporate position. Besides, unless you count going before the board of my SEAL Unit, I hadn't been in a job interview since I was in high school.

They flew me in early one morning and had a car waiting to drive me into downtown Salt Lake City. I was dressed in my best suit, trying to look as professional as possible. I arrived at their headquarters and was told that my interview wouldn't be for another three hours. Needing to kill some time, I found a place to eat breakfast at a mall on the city's main drag. I then wandered into a bookstore and meandered around until I found myself in the religion section. The waiting game was stressing me out, and I needed something to calm me down before the interview.

I scanned the titles, looking for something that grabbed my attention. Somehow, I spotted a tiny book wedged among the others and was drawn to it. I pried it off the shelf to take a look. I wish that I could remember the title. The table of contents was basically a list of things to pray for. There were passages on wisdom, on courage, on success. I probably spent an hour reading verses under my breath that applied to my situation. Soon, I felt calm, confident, and relaxed.

When it was time for my interview, I walked into the conference room ready for anything. I was told that one of the partners was planning to sit in on my presentation along with the other individuals on the panel. I was the last candidate of the four and, so I was told, the partners hadn't been present for anyone else's interview. The partner was obviously a busy man, because he ate his lunch while I made my pitch.

Each candidate had been given a predetermined set of questions to research and answer, and I'd done my due diligence to ensure that I was prepared. I had a PowerPoint presentation ready to go, and I was just getting started when he stopped me. "We've heard all of this before," the partner said. There was a disadvantage to being last, and his comment threw me off my plan. For a second, I panicked. I took a deep breath and fell back on what I knew best. I spoke from the heart.

Shortly into my pitch, the partner invited me to sit down and get comfortable. What had been scheduled to be a fifteen-minute session turned into an hour-and-a-half discussion. The company does a lot of business in Central America, and our conversation quickly migrated to the cartels. They asked me how I would respond to various contingencies, and I systematically led them through my thought process. I immediately felt at home among these professionals, and on the way out, one of them pulled me aside and let me know how well he thought I'd done. He probably told every candidate the same thing, but it felt good nonetheless.

It was a couple of weeks before I heard anything; I was checking my phone and my email impatiently every few minutes. The longer I waited, the more I second-guessed my performance. Every time I thought about it, though, I knew that I'd done my best. I was either the right candidate or I wasn't. At long last, the call came: the contract was mine.

I was elated. I now had a firm plan for my future, one that would ensure that I was able to take care of my family. In no time I was doing risk assessments of their operations and locations and improving their readiness overall. My work with them quickly led to other contracts, and I soon found myself with a nice stable of clients.

If I could establish myself as a resource in Central America, I knew that I would never have a shortage of business. I worked every lead that I could, calling on friends back at my SEAL Unit and other government agencies as resources. The key would be to have someone on the ground down south, someone whose network could provide real-time intelligence. It took several trips south before I found the right in-country partners. They were totally wired in, giving me access to valuable resources and cultural experience that I was still developing. As my footprint grew, so did my marketability. Because of the company's growth, I renamed it Contingent Group, which better represented our team approach.

HOT WASH

Find your life's passion. Do work that is meaningful to you, whether it is lucrative or not. If you do what you love you will be successful, and the financial aspects will take care of themselves.

I strongly believe in multiple sources of income. Not only did I have my military retirement income in addition to Contingent Group, I sought out additional opportunities to build a financial cushion. As we learned during COVID, you can never depend on anything 100 percent of the time. The more diversified your income streams, the safer you will be when things don't go as planned. Think of them as layers of security.

You can prepare, prepare, prepare, but always be ready to adjust and go with the flow. My ability to be flexible when forced to abandon my presentation got me the job and changed the course of my life. That flexibility came with confidence born of years of real-world experience. No amount of research can replace that.

FINDING BOTTOM

I settled into married life and poured myself into Contingent Group, which I viewed as my family's future. The income stream that I'd created was a huge boost to our family's finances, since living on an enlisted military salary had not exactly been lavish.

Building a new business takes capital, and I did not want to put myself into debt or take on investors. In the coordinator position, I was more or less operating on autopilot, so I began the process of steadily building my company and its infrastructure. Contingent Group would have an international focus, which meant that travel was a necessity. My thinking was that, if I worked hard setting things up correctly now, life would be better later on. As it turned out, Anna didn't agree with my vision. What should have been a happy and exciting time in my life became anything but.

Central America is home to some of the most dangerous countries on earth, but its proximity to the US and deep connection with the US economy means that American businessmen need to sometimes travel south of the border. These are exactly the types of missions that Contingent Group was specializing in, and so it was important that I spent time on the ground down south before I ever brought a client down. My reputation was on the line, which meant that our operations had to be set up to my own personal standard; that meant that I had to be there, away from home. This was an investment in our family's future and, like any investment, there was some sacrifice and risk on the front end.

Although I thought this had all been discussed and settled, Anna began complaining about being responsible for my kids when I was traveling, which was often for weeks at a time. We argued, we fought, and within months I'd had enough. I knew what a bad marriage looked like, and I wasn't going to do this again.

I wanted out, so I made a plan. I didn't want to fight about leaving, so I decided that I would just tear off the bandage. I met with a realtor and found a rental house a mile or so down the road from Anna, so that my kids' lives wouldn't be disrupted more than necessary. One morning, Anna went to work and the kids went to school. By the time school was over, I'd moved all of our belongings, and my kids came home to a new house. Anna was not amused.

Months went by; we decided to give it one more chance. Trust me, I know what you're thinking; I've never claimed to be a fast learner when it comes to my personal life. We moved our collective families into a giant 5,500-square-foot house, which was plenty of room for all of us. She wanted to buy the home together, but I still had my doubts about the future of our relationship, so I hedged my bets with a lease-purchase option.

Our change of scenery didn't fix our problems. I wish that I could say that I wasn't part of the problem, but the fact is that I was still difficult to get close to. My travel didn't slow down either, which led us right back into the fights that had driven me away before. I moved out yet again, this time for good.

Despite all of the good things that were happening career-wise, it was during this time that I hit my low point. My relationship had failed, and whatever happiness that Tulsa had represented soon became darkness.

Something in my head wasn't right. I wouldn't sleep for several days at a time and would finally collapse, exhausted. I'd wake up and repeat the cycle of insomnia for a few more days. I was back to drinking nearly every night, since that helped me go to sleep—though in reality I was just passing out from the booze. I took whatever pills that I could get a hold of. It was bad.

When I did sleep, I'd have vivid nightmares: I was always killing people or they were trying to kill me. Those were the types of dreams that feel incredibly real. I would wake up, either terrified or satisfied, and it would take me a few moments to realize that I was home safe in my bed. One night I had a particularly bad dream where I was being pursued by some demonic creature. I was jolted awake, and as I lurched upward in bed, I put out my palm in a defensive posture and yelled "Jesus!" The open bathroom door was directly in front of my bed. Just as I spoke His name, the rack that held all of my soap and shampoo broke free from the shower wall and crashed to the floor with a bang. That rack had never fallen before and never did again. It was eerie.

My faith wasn't a light switch to happiness, though. When I wasn't busy with work or the kids, I would often go to a dark place mentally. The stress of getting out of the military, finding new ways of providing for my family, and facing the failure of another marriage seemed like insurmountable hurdles. I was terrified of the future.

My mind became consumed with those thoughts, and one day, I decided that enough was enough. For the first time in my life, I was ready to quit. I'd endured the toughest training and selection events that the military had to offer, but the combined weight of my fears and stresses had me wanting to ring the bell on life. It was around noon, and my kids were all in school, leaving me alone with my painful past and my uncertain future. As I sat on the bed with my bare feet on the floor, my eyes moved toward the nightstand where my handgun spent every night. A voice inside me said *Yeah, that's right, this is a way.* There had been no premeditation; it simply came over me in the moment. It was like being in a trance.

The handgun was a 9mm SIG SAUER P228, a slightly more compact version of the pistol I'd carried my entire career. I picked it up and felt its familiar comfort. I laid the gun on my thigh, with my trigger finger resting alongside the frame. Here it was: the solution to all my problems. I knew that shooting myself through the eyeball would be an instant and painless death, having seen so many terrorists collapse like wet noodles from that shot. It was over; I was checking out.

Thoughts raced through my head in a fast-forward blur. *Should I do it? Should I not do it? Should I go back to Anna? Should I go back to Cincinnati?* I was actively debating the pros and cons of putting a jacketed hollow-point bullet through my brain. Tears rolled down my cheeks. The crying wasn't emotional; it was physical.

Before I could turn the muzzle toward my face, I found myself looking down from above, picturing the image of taking my own life. My brains were sprayed across the room, and a puddle of blood surrounded my lifeless body. I thought about my children coming home from a carefree day at school, still wearing their backpacks as they excitedly opened the door to my bedroom. I pictured them finding their father's body in a lifeless heap on the floor, an image that would haunt them until their deaths. The thought of my children seeing this jolted me from my dark thoughts. I put down the gun and began to sob. *What was I doing?* My heart raced as I snapped out of it.

Instantly, I was furious at myself for even considering suicide, and I cursed the devil for leading me down that path. I had never for a moment considered taking my own life before that day, and it has not crossed my mind since. What had gotten into me? All I can think about now are those who, in that moment, ended it all. I needed to get the fuck out of my house, so I chose the only real therapy that I'd ever known. I walked out the door and headed to the gym. I spent the rest of the day shaking my head in disbelief at what I'd almost done.

HOT WASH

Everything in your life can be classified as either an asset or a liability. Assets are the things that make you better and lift you up; liabilities are the elements that drag you down. Bad relationships can be a liability, as can toxic work environments, friends, and addictions. When the liabilities stack up against you, you're going to be overloaded. Identify these liabilities, methodically remove them from your life, and your situation will improve.

Before that day, I had always believed that suicide was a coward's way out. Taking the gift of your own life is the most selfish act imaginable. Doing so destroys your loved ones' lives instantly. Now that I've been in that place, though, I understand the pain and the hopelessness that can drive someone to consider suicide. Life will get better if you let it. Once you pull that trigger or swallow those pills, there is no turning back. As the saying goes, "it is a permanent solution to a temporary problem."

To everyone who is reading this and struggling, especially my brother and sister veterans, call someone, ask someone for help, get on your knees and pray. Just don't take away that precious gift. **You are not alone, and you are worth it! We owe it to those who didn't make it home to live our lives to the fullest**.

TURNING THE PAGE

W hether it was due to the traumatic brain injuries caused by so many explosive breaches or was some type of PTSD, my head wasn't right. I would sit down to try and do some office work and would end up pacing relentlessly, unable to focus. This mental state was not conducive to running a successful business with so many moving parts. According to the Concussion Legacy Foundation, "Early symptoms of Chronic Traumatic Encephalopathy (CTE) usually appear in a patient's late twenties or thirties, and affect a patient's mood and behavior. Some common changes seen include impulse control problems, aggression, depression, and paranoia," exactly the behaviors that I'd displayed during my failed relationship with Anna.

I began hearing about a place that was helping veterans, particularly SEALs, deal with the negative effects that combat and training had inflicted on our brains. It was called the Cerebrum Health Centers, and it was located down in Dallas, Texas. A friend told me about it when I first moved to Tulsa, but I brushed it off. Finally, my condition worsened to the point that I had to seriously consider it.

My BUD/S roommate Joe was being treated there, as were other Teams guys that I knew. All of them reported excellent results, and there was even a liaison who helped bring SEALS in for treatment at no cost, thanks to a nonprofit foundation. My depression and inability to sleep or concentrate were really taking their toll, and I knew it was time to give this a try.

I'm glad that I did. There are two events that I credit with turning my post-deployment life around: finding Christ, and receiving excellent care at the Centers.

I made the trip down to Dallas and was immediately impressed with the operation; these guys were pros. It was an intensive two-week program: first, diagnosis, and then a variety of treatments. Technicians scanned my brain using electrodes and imaging techniques to establish a baseline of the various lobes and how they were functioning. Without getting too technical, they applied several therapies to help my brain heal, effectively retraining it. Since blood flow to parts of my brain had been diminished, they strapped me into a gyroscopic chair that would turn my body sideways and upside down. This inversion therapy used gravity to force blood into some of the damaged areas of my brain.

There were a number of brain exercises, including a variety of video-based memory drills. Some of them reminded me of "Kim's

Game," from the 1901 Rudyard Kipling espionage novel *Kim*. In the book, a young would-be spy is briefly shown a tray full of objects. After the tray is removed, he must describe the items in detail. I learned that the human brain is a simply amazing organ, capable of a tremendous amount if properly stimulated. We did exercises of that type for hours each day; it was exhausting. Just as someone who had never exercised their body would be shocked after a workout, I was giving my brain a workout for the first time. As soon as the treatments were done for the day, I would walk back to the hotel and crash.

I've since learned that the Centers' treatment methods were considered controversial and its finances suspect. It is no longer in operation. All I know is that what they did worked wonders for me. The process was challenging, but the results were almost immediate. My sleep improved dramatically, and I regained my ability to focus. Soon I was sleeping seven to nine hours a night, which was unheard of for me. On my first day back in the office after my trip to Dallas, I sat down and worked for six hours straight. I felt as though I'd taken Adderall or Ritalin, I was so focused. I finally took a break only because I was too hungry to keep working. The timing of my treatment was perfect, because it would soon be time to build Contingent Group full time.

I was set to leave the Navy, but I had one last mission to complete. On March 18, 2016, Utah's governor signed legislation establishing the Chief Special Warfare Operator (SEAL) Jason R. Workman Memorial Bridge. With only a few weeks left on active duty before my terminal leave began, I traveled back to southern Utah to honor my friend. Surrounded by the high red cliffs that Jason explored as a kid, a green-and-white metal sign bearing his name was unveiled.

The bridge, which spans the San Juan River near Mexican Hat, is on US Route 163, fifty miles south of his hometown of Blanding. I still think about Jason every day, but being back alongside his friends and family five years after his death helped me put that dark chapter of my life behind me.

On August 31, 2016, I officially retired from the military. It was, in a word, terrifying. Despite my extensive combat experience, there is almost a child-like innocence among career military people when it comes to many aspects of the civilian world. Everything from a steady paycheck to health insurance had been covered for me since I was seventeen years old, and now the responsibility for it all fell on my shoulders. I felt nervous, almost the way I'd felt as a kid when I went to a new school. I honestly think that it's this part that so many veterans struggle with—as a society and as a military, we need to do a better job of smoothing out this transition.

I didn't know the other recruiters and they didn't know me, so I opted out of having a retirement party locally. My SEAL brothers were still in the fight, still on that train that never stops. There was no pomp or circumstance; one day I was a special warfare operator chief petty officer in the United States Navy, and the next I was just Eddie. I'd be lying if I didn't admit that I felt a little bit adrift.

With my relationship with Anna over, I needed to make arrangements for someone to help with my kids, since I still needed to travel. I had no support system in Oklahoma. My mother, God bless her, offered to step in. With no reason to stay in Tulsa, I made the move back to Cincinnati a few days after my retirement. All three kids were visiting their mother so, once again, they came home to a new home in a new city with new schools and friends to make. If someone writes a book about my children, it should be entitled *Resilient*.

Margarita time with mom celebrating my retirement.
After 20 years, we finally get to have a "normal" relationship.

I rented a house in Cincinnati and picked up right where I'd left off with Contingent Group. My mom threw me a retirement party, and friends of mine from high school, the Marine Corps, and the Teams all came to celebrate. My childhood buddy Oz from the neighborhood even showed up. It was really cool to come full circle and be back where I'd started, alongside so many good people that life's path had introduced me to.

TOP: Attempting to play golf with the Laverty Lane crew—me, Chad (left), and Oz (right). We left our spears at home this time. BOTTOM: (Left to right) Little Murph, Mr. Murphy, Dad, and me at a Cincinnati Reds game in 2017.

At some point I sat down with my dad and flat out asked him if he thought he'd done a good job as a father. I didn't ask the question in order to put him down or challenge him; I asked it because I was struggling as a father and sought his guidance. He didn't hesitate—he simply said "no." I could see the sadness in his eyes. (For the record, I think that on the whole he was a great father, and I told him so, but he did have some shortcomings.)

The very things that my dad had struggled with—drinking, wild behavior, and toxic relationships—had all become a part of my life. I had become the very thing that I'd despised, failing where he had failed. I made the decision that I had to break the cycle for the sake of my own kids. I had to step up, had to do better.

All grown up, me and my girls.

Part of that process would be moving on. A few months after I arrived in Cincinnati, my divorce with Anna was finalized. It was more or less simple and amicable since it was a second marriage for both of us. Though it didn't work out between us, I have nothing but good things to say about Anna. I was the toxic element in our marriage, not she. Anna is a kind and decent person who led me to Christ when I needed him most. That action alone probably saved my life.

With that relationship behind me, it was time to get to work.

▪ ▪ ▪

My meeting was with a local police official. Most law enforcement activity and personnel of the border are controlled by the various drug cartels and, though this man was no exception, he was pretty honest by local standards. One of my clients would soon be conducting business in the area, and it was important that we had the blessing of the local police and, by proxy, the cartels. Having done my homework, I knew that a gift was appropriate for such a meeting, so I had bought a nice pair of Ray-Ban sunglasses to bring along.

The scene unfolded like something out of a bad movie. We sat on the patio of a local restaurant, overlooking the crystal blue waters of the Gulf of California. The chief was around my own age, dressed in an open-collared button-down shirt and slacks. We each had our own interpreter, and the four of us settled into our seats.

I slid the Ray-Bans across the table and watched as he nodded in acknowledgment of the gift. I explained that my clients were involved in a commercial construction project that was being guarded by his officers. A competitor firm to my client had paid locals to disrupt the project, essentially employing paid protestors, to make life difficult. Someone was paying the cops, too, and so they stood by and let the agitators do their thing.

The chief listened intently as the interpreter conveyed the information, his face betraying nothing. He paused for a moment in contemplation before speaking. He would exchange all of the security guards for new men who weren't on the competitor's payroll. Our project could move forward as scheduled; my client was pleased. No guns were drawn, no shots fired, no force was necessary. I had become a "fixer." My knowledge of the local culture, built using my own intelligence network, had solved the problem with minimal drama.

Enjoying family time with Mom and my stepdad, Rick.

I made dozens of trips, solving problems for my clients and ensuring their safety. I traveled back and forth between Cincinnati and Central America, balancing my dual roles as father and business owner, trying to prevent my mother from carrying too heavy a burden.

Throughout my career I'd always wanted to return to Cincinnati; it was my home. A few months in, though, it became obvious that absence had made the heart grow fonder, and that in reality it wasn't the city of my dreams.

Back when I was in Dallas getting my brain unrattled, I'd fallen in love with Texas. I liked everything about it: the people were great, the patriotic culture put me at ease, and the tax laws were ideal for a small business owner. Texas was also far closer to Central America than Cincinnati; I could get direct flights out of Dallas-Fort Worth to numerous cities in Mexico and beyond. That meant less time away from home.

With my old teammate, Dom Raso. Always take care of those who have your back.

Kailha's high school graduation. After the ceremony,
we jumped into my truck and moved to Texas.

After about eight months in Cincinnati, I decided that it was time to move, this time to a city outside of Dallas. Kailha was in her senior year of high school and I didn't want to disrupt her at such a crucial time in her life, so we waited until the summer began. I was filled with pride as I watched her cross the stage and receive her diploma (despite the fact that she was graduating from my high school's rival). That little girl who had crawled up onto my chest, dragging her blanket behind her, was now a woman.

The car was already packed and, after the ceremony, Sammie, Triston, and I drove straight to Texas. We were moving yet again but, this time, it was permanent.

HOT WASH

I'd spent my adult life in an environment where seeking help was seen as a sign of weakness. That mindset, combined with pure laziness, allowed me to delay getting the treatment that my mind needed. **Don't wait until things get out of hand before seeking help; doing so doesn't make you weak, it makes you smart**.

It's no different from what clinicians call referred pain. This is when an injury in one area of the body causes pain in another. I'm told that it is often brought on by a delay in treatment. My lack of sleep affected my work and my fitness level, which in turn altered my mood for the worse. My bad mood strained my relationships and my parenting. It's not just the issue itself; it is all of the follow-on problems that can also consume you and drag you down.

There was nothing magic about my meeting with the police chief in Mexico. I didn't have a great sales pitch or a bag of cash with which to grease the wheels—everything was above board. I was simply courteous and respectful of his role and of his culture. Sometimes politely asking for what you need is the best path to achieving it. Always know the local rules and act accordingly. Doing my research and learning the local customs made the difference between success and failure for both me and my client. Information is invaluable, but only if you use it.

AT LAST, PEACE

The drive from the airport outside of Geneva, New York, into town was short and picturesque. Located upstate, on one of the Empire State's famed Finger Lakes, Geneva has a population of around twelve thousand. It's the home to Hobart and William Smith Colleges, coordinate institutions for men and women. Hobart was founded in 1822 and sits on a 320acre joint campus.

Hobart is, in many ways, the archetypical liberal arts college of the northeast: small, expensive, and academically competitive. It looks the part, too, with stone buildings that date back to the campus' early days. It seemed to me like a place where Harry Potter might walk by at any moment.

I'd been asked to speak to Hobart's trainee athletes, which was an honor. As a young athlete, I had been greatly influenced by the words of men like Coach Lyons. I was proud to pay it forward and continue that tradition.

Though I'd earned my degree, I'd done it mostly online and had never gotten a taste of the traditional college experience: no fraternity parties, no Saturday football games. My true education had been acquired in some of the least forgiving classrooms imaginable. My campuses were Parris Island, Coronado, and Virginia Beach; the mountains of Afghanistan, and the streets of Iraq. My professors were ruthless Marine drill sergeants, SEAL BUD/S instructors, and suicidal insurgents. My coaches were the older teammates who mentored me along the way.

I hoped that, despite our different backgrounds, I would be able to connect with the trainees. While I'd fought and watched my friends die, most of these kids had likely led nice, sheltered, and peaceful lives.

I parked the compact rental car and said a silent prayer, asking God to give me the strength and wisdom to motivate these young men to do their very best on the field and in life. Though Hobart is small in terms of enrollment, its athletic footprint is impressive. When I walked into the auditorium, the seats were filled with hundreds of young, fit individuals from the school's various intercollegiate sports: football, basketball, hockey, lacrosse, and others. No swimmers, unfortunately.

After an introduction by a school official, I took the stage and began my motivational speech. I've given a number of such presentations to various groups, and though I don't have a canned script, most follow the same basic outline:

My focus is mindset since, in my experience, it is the single most important element of life. You often cannot control your situation, but you can control your mind—something that I first learned in the sand pits of Parris Island.

Mindset is everything. There is not a barrier that cannot be overcome with the correct attitude. In 1964, Jim Marshall was a defensive end for the Minnesota Vikings. During the first half of a game, Marshall recovered the opposing team's fumble. Excited, he ran the wrong way and into the opposite end zone. He scored two points for the other team and, since it had been a safety, they got the ball as well. It was the kind of thing every athlete has nightmares about, something that would haunt you for years.

The fans booed, the coaches yelled, and his teammates undoubtedly treated him like a toxic chemical. But Marshall didn't quit, didn't feel sorry for himself, and didn't make excuses. In the second half, he had the game of his life. He made multiple tackles and sacks, caused a fumble, and almost single-handedly changed the course of the game. His team won. He didn't become a bitter athlete in the second half; he just got his head in the right place. Challenges are 90 percent mental. This is true in sports, in combat, and in life. It was true for me in the Marine Corps, the SEAL Teams, as a single father, and when I battled my internal demons.

Choices. Every single day there are and will be choices for each of us, as an individual, to make. As miniscule as they may seem at the time, those choices will determine your life's journey. You will no doubt make the wrong choices in life at some times and the right ones at other times. You have free will, so choose wisely.

"Can't" should not be a word in your vocabulary. I heard it often in BUD/S: "I can't do that; the water is too cold." Those individuals soon left. The water was no warmer for me than it was for those quitters. People ask all the time about workouts to prepare for BUD/S: running, swimming, push-ups, pull-ups, sit-ups. Should I lift weights? Should I bulk up? Should I sleep deprive myself? Should I take cold showers? I often laugh, and then I simply explain that it is almost 100 percent in your MIND. The human brain is one of the most amazing and devastating things I have ever seen and experienced. Use it for good, and your goals will be attained.

Heart. I have seen the strongest and fastest of men crumble when the heart, the passion, and the want is put to the test. They can turn to a wad of cookie dough really quickly when they are out of their element and their inner workings are exposed. I have also seen the smallest and slowest of men show the heart of a lion when times are tough. The unforeseen changes that happen within our bodies when we have a goal is a beautiful sight to see. I saw it in many fellow classmates in BUD/S and throughout my career. I see it in certain business executives, and I do my best to teach it to my children. Heart and mindset go hand in hand and, together, they are the key to any accomplishment.

Influencers. We all have them, and often those who influence us do not know it. When I watched my dad unhesitatingly jump into the lake to retrieve an anchor, he influenced me deeply. He did not talk about it; he saw a job that needed to be done and he did it. That one act, that maybe lasted a total of thirty seconds, stayed with me through all of my training. I can still see it to this day. The point is that you never know who is watching, and you can be the difference-maker in someone's life. This can be for the good and unfortunately for the bad, so always strive to do the right thing.

Be an asset. On a team, in your family, and elsewhere in life you have two options: to be an asset or a liability. The asset is the person people can count on in any given situation. The liability is the one people cannot depend on. There is no in between!

Don't be afraid of failure. Try, and even if you fail, you will learn from the experience. Had I not failed to qualify for sniper school, I would have never left the Marines. I would have never made the friends that I made or had the experiences that I did. I didn't realize it at the time, but failing to achieve my dream was part of the plan.

One of my greatest mentors was a command master chief at my SEAL Unit, who will remain nameless. I closed my speech with his rules for life. I have learned that by following these rules, your life—both professional and personal—will be much better. For me, it is not enough to float through life. I want and need to do my best and hopefully inspire others along the way, paying forward what I received. Mentors like him shaped my path, a path where mistakes were learned from and were never to be repeated.

Be aggressive in whatever you do. If you want it, you make it happen. No "but," no "I'll do it later"—get off your ass and make it happen. Want it, find a way, and be able to look back and think to yourself, *I just owned that obstacle. What's next?* Then *repeat the cycle.*

Look cool. Regardless of where I go or what I do, I try to look respectable. I'm not talking about having the coolest clothes or shades, although that's not frowned upon. The point is to never look like a slob. No matter what you are told, you are judged on first appearances. We never know when those occasions may be, so always look the part. Even when I go to the gym, I like my clothes to match; my hair looks good, or I have a crisp hat on my head. It is not vanity—I am getting ready for battle, getting ready to better myself. We perform better when we feel better, and some of that comes from how we perceive ourselves. Why not do your part and look good? It will affect your performance in a positive way.

Be deliberate in your actions. When you're in the aisle of the grocery store, you move right to avoid another shopper. Then they move the same direction, and you change course. The awkward dance continues. If you'd simply made a choice and stuck with it, the situation could be avoided. Have a goal. Be deliberate on how to get there. The quickest way between two points is a straight line; be deliberate in making your line.

Act like you own the place. Carry yourself with confidence, no matter what you feel inside. Not cocky, but confident. If you look like a slob (see **Look cool**), you'll have to prove otherwise. If you look sharp, the opposite will be true. When you walk into a room, own it. Keep your head high and greet strangers warmly. A "hi" or "how are you" goes a long way. Greeting others gives the impression that you belong and are not an outsider. Where you go, what you do is your world, so act like it.

Do the right thing. This can be the most challenging, since we are all human and prone to selfishness and, yes, to PRIDE. Integrity is doing the right thing when no one is watching, and without integrity, there can be no trust. Without trust, there is no team. Humble yourself, say sorry when you are wrong, help others when they are in need. Pick up that piece of trash that someone so carelessly threw on the ground. We always hear people wanting change. You want change? Then be the change. It starts with you—it starts now.

Implementation. We all have great ideas. Talk is cheap; action is what matters. You want to impress? You want to stand out? Be the person who implements what you think and speak. Be a doer, not a talker. Don't talk about writing a book, learning Jiujitsu, or learning to play guitar—do it.

The power of the team. While you must be driven from within, you will be stronger and more effective as part of a determined group. During the darkest moments of BUD/S, my boat crew mates filled me with their positive energy. We were all determined, but we fed off one another. I wanted to perform better for them, and they did for me. The team is true success!

After the *two*-hour-long presentation and conclusion of the event, many of the athletes made their way over to where I was standing. A number of them thanked me for my service, which is always nice, and I did my best to answer any questions they had.

The predictable questions about BUD/S were the most common, but some surprised me. One of the trainee athletes, a fit football player, asked me whether I thought it was disrespectful to kneel during the national anthem. This was at the beginning of the NFL kneeling controversy. I made it clear that I found it to be highly disrespectful of the flag and those who have sacrificed for it. He pushed back, somewhat adamantly, that this was an expression of liberty and part of our freedom of speech.

I asked him to take a step back and look at the big picture. Children look up to athletes and can be heavily influenced by them. These players are setting an example that patriotism is somehow offensive, which in the long run is detrimental to the very fabric of our nation. He shook his head, dismissive of my position. It struck me that he didn't really want to hear my answer as much as he wanted to ask the question.

I took a breath and began telling him about my friend Jason. I talked about how Jason had fought bravely for that flag, for that anthem. His demeaner changed noticeably when I talked about President Obama standing at attention, saluting that flag while the bodies of Jason and thirty other Americans were offloaded at Dover. Then I told him about looking at Jason's son Jax during the funeral, a little boy whose only tangible connection to his father will be the folded American flag on the family's mantle. How will it make him feel when he sees our society's icons take a knee as that flag waves?

The conversation ended there, and he was respectful enough not to press further. I have no idea whether I gave him food for thought, but we had a civil conversation—something that is missing from today's society. If we are to survive as a nation, we must learn again to respect one another, even when we don't see eye to eye.

HOT WASH

I have had so many mentors, leaders, and friends that I have looked up to and taken key leadership traits from. These men and women gave back, passing on their wisdom, knowledge, and experiences. I too hope that I can influence the upcoming generation, as those individuals did me. I believe it is what we are called to do. Make the ones who are younger and less experienced better than you when it is all said and done. This is how we improve as humans, as a team, and as a nation.

NEW BEGINNINGS

B ack at home in Dallas, I met a beautiful, hilarious young woman named Amanda at (where else?) the gym. She had grown up in the area and actually gone to high school with my late buddy Millsy. Like me, Amanda was divorced, and she was raising her two children. We clicked instantly. I know what you're thinking: another relationship? This one is different... *honestly.* All of my previous relationships had physical rather than emotional foundations. I'd finally learned that turning a hookup into a marriage was not a recipe for success.

Amanda and I developed a friendship over the course of two full years before we ever took things in a romantic direction. We would chat briefly in the gym, and sometimes those little conversations would turn into longer, deeper ones. Ironically, we gave one another a great deal of relationship advice. We would rarely see one another outside of that setting, but we did take some walks in the park together. Yes, kids: even in the age of social media and constant digital connection, a simple walk in the park can be a life-changing experience.

We continued to be friends but, at some point, things shifted. It hit me that I wanted this to be more than a friendship and, fortunately for me,

It took me a while, but I found my perfect mate. Never quit and learn from our mistakes!

it hit her too. We had a mature, frank discussion regarding our future and committed to being exclusive with one another. Once things took that turn, we began dating, and after the drama of my past, I could truly appreciate the quiet ease of our relationship. Our respective families quickly fell in with one another.

Mother's Day came around and I wanted Amanda to know how we all felt about her. I wanted to make the day special for her, something that had never been her ex's priority. We made plans to have brunch at my house after she spent the morning with her children. The kids and I cleaned the house, spent the morning in the kitchen, and even typed up menus. I put on my best suit, Triston did the same, and Sammie put on a nice dress.

Celebrating Halloween with some good ole fashioned cultural appropriation.

Amanda had no idea that we had done any of this. I met her outside the house, and as soon as she saw how I was dressed, I could tell that she was moved. She didn't make it out of the car before she began to tear up. I took her by the arm and walked her inside, where Triston was waiting. He stood in the hallway, wearing his suit and characteristic grin, greeting her with a single red rose. Amanda took her usual seat by the fireplace, and Sammie served her appetizers and a mimosa before handing over our custom Mother's Day brunch menu.

We sat smiling together at the table and had a great meal of shrimp, crab, pancakes, eggs, and, Amanda's favorite, filet mignon. Sammie baked her phenomenal homemade muffins. I wished that Kailha had been there, but she had taken her own life's journey and was now a mother herself. That's right, the little girl who'd climbed onto my chest during BUD/S now had a child of her own. At the end of the meal, there was one more surprise.

Unknown in advance to me, Sammie stood up, pulled out a letter to Amanda, and read it aloud in front of all of us. I had no idea where she was going with this. The letter started out slowly, and by the end, we were all in tears. I could hardly believe that such amazing words had come from the heart of a teenager. I was floored, tears dripping down my cheeks, and looking over at Amanda, she was in no better shape. Even though it wasn't about me, hearing these words made me feel immensely proud.

As a single father, failure was a daily occurrence. I tried to be the best parent that I could be, but no matter how hard I tried, I could not be a mother. All I wanted for my children was a good female figure in their lives; someone to look up to. A mentor. That dream had finally come true. There is no other way to put it—I struck gold with Amanda. My children and I were and are thankful.

Triston had the only dry eyes, simply because he was too young to understand the feelings and emotions swarming around that room. Amanda and I got up and hugged Sammie, telling her how much that letter meant, and that we loved her. We sat back down as Sammie said to me, "I know this is Mother's Day, but we will celebrate you too, being that you play the mom and dad for us." She pulled out another letter. I was already overwhelmed with emotions, something that I've always struggled to express. I was a mess and now she was going in for round two. She started the letter, and it read:

Happy Mother's Day

Happy mother's day to my amazing father. You are insane. You were the father and mother role in Kaihla's, Triston's & my life. Not many people could do this, but you could! I love knowing that I have the best dad in the universe.

My dad was in the military for years & survived through
it all without getting a single bullet to touch his body. My
dad is strong. Now I'm not talking about just physically, my
dad is also strong mentaly. My dad has the best mindset,
he knows what he needs to do to achive his dreams. My
dad knows how to keep his family safe & happy. My dad
is unique. He has several tattoos but there's more. My
father is a big kid. He will watch any marvel of xman
movie, he will play any black ops with you, and if you feel
like playing dark hide n seek one night he will gladly
scare you while playing. My dad has done so much. He
took care of all 3 of his children when his youngest was
only a few months old. Yes I have an idea of how stressful
this could have been but my dad tried his best which
is all that matters. So maybe he didn't know how to do
my sisters nor my hair. Or maybe he didn't know how to
cook that well, but he did know how to make us happy
even in the darkest of times. My dad is one of the
greatest things in my life & has been for 16 years. Yes
we may argue sometimes but who doesn't argue with
their parents?

The fact that my kids have been through so much, yet are
so well adjusted, is a testament to the resilience of humanity.
Between my being absent for a good portion of their childhood,
the toxic relationships they've witnessed, and having had to be
the new kids at school far too many times, they have had every
excuse to fail. They've refused. I wish I could take credit for their
strengths, but that would be doing them a disservice. I spent most

of my life chasing my dream job, not knowing that the greatest job on the planet is to be a parent. I'm eternally grateful that I finally realized it.

How time flies, my daughter Kailha's wedding day.

✳ ✳ ✳

There is a postscript to this story, one that happened just as I was finishing this book. Amanda and I took a trip to the Grand Tetons and Yellowstone, a part of this amazing nation that neither of us had ever seen. In the shadow of the breathtaking beauty of the Tetons, I stopped Amanda and turned to look into her eyes. With the blessing of our children and Amanda's mother, and after a million and one prayers to God, I got on one knee and asked Amanda to marry me. She said *yes!* With her family and mine, we are a whole. Despite all the odds, I have found happiness, peace, a Savior, and now a life companion: I've found my best friend. There is light after darkness.

As a child of divorce and someone who struggled with relationships, I never had the family that I envisioned. I tried to force it and often filled the void with my career. My teammates became my family. Now, after spending time with Amanda and the melting pot that is our family tribe, I recognize that I am finally where I've always wanted to be. At last, I am at peace, and it is the greatest feeling that I have ever experienced.

We'd had a public wedding planned for a future date, but for various reasons decided to go down to the courthouse to make our marriage legal. We wore nice but casual clothes, and it was a simple yet incredibly meaningful process. Afterward, we decided to go to a nice dinner at a local Italian restaurant to celebrate.

Triston happened to be the only child in town, so I sent him a text asking what he wanted us to bring him from the restaurant's menu. Typical of his palate, he chose a seafood dish called Capellini alla Pescatora: clams, mussels, shrimp, and calamari over angel hair pasta—not exactly kid food. Of course, his choice was one of the most expensive items on the menu. Ordinarily I would have gone right for the steaks, but his chosen seafood medley sounded really good. I ordered the dish and Amanda ordered chicken; our plan was to share each with one another.

She said yes! Moments after proposing to my wife, Amanda. Love you baby.

We had a couple of drinks and talked about our new life together. I'd been a guest on a podcast the evening before, during which we had discussed my career, my faith, this book project, and Contingent Group. Amanda told me that it bothered her that I constantly have to talk about my past, particularly the painful elements. I understood and appreciated her position, but I told her that talking about that past was part of appreciating the present. Without the mistakes, the failures, the ignorance, and the sin, there's no meaning to the redemption.

Our food arrived and everything was perfect. I bit into one of the clams and immediately felt something hard against my teeth. I'm a fat kid at heart, and I love food way too much to waste it. I ate around the foreign object until I'd devoured every edible morsel. Whatever was left in my mouth felt like it was going to crack one of my molars, so I put my napkin to my face and stealthily spit out the offending object. It took me a moment to realize what it was—my clam had contained an almost perfect white pearl! It looked like it had come right out of a jewelry store showroom.

I had no idea that clams could even produce a pearl, and according to what I've read it is incredibly rare to find one, especially one of this color and shape. Some basic internet research confirmed that this round, white pearl appears less than once for every ten thousand clams. Digging deeper, I looked into the symbolism of the pearl. Here is what I discovered:

*According to history and the myths, pearls are symbolic of **wisdom gained through experience**. These gems are believed to offer protection, as well as to attract good luck and wealth. They are well-known for their calming effects. Pearls have a way of bringing balance to your karma.*

Myths have it that pearls keep your children safe while strengthening your relationships. It is also said that these little gemstones are symbolic of the wearer's loyalty, generosity, integrity, and purity.

I no longer believe in eerie coincidences. At the darkest and most dire moments in my life, these moments had occurred. I'd heard an unexplainable voice the night Luis was killed, and I saw the "SAVED" sign when I questioned whether my sins could be forgiven. To me, the pearl was another such event. I took it as a wedding gift and a message from God that, so long as we put Him first, He would take care of us. A pat on the head confirming that we are on the right path. I was overcome with emotion. I was crying, Amanda was crying, we even called our moms and they both started crying.

Finding Christ and doing my best to surrender all to Him was, and is, the greatest blessing of my life. Our family makes every attempt to put God first and make the right choices. As I sit here and type these words, tears roll down my cheeks. They are tears of happiness for what God can do and will do when you let Him. Remember that things work on His timing, not our own, so understand and respect that. Be patient. We still fail, but we learn and continue to get stronger.

I'm not going to pretend that I live in some utopian fantasy world where everything is perfect all of the time. We still have our daily struggles; the failures and stresses of life are a constant. We deal with the demands of work, wrestle with family issues, and both try to maintain cordial relationships with our respective exes for the sake of our children. Life is not easy, but with the knowledge that there is a God above and Amanda is by my side, the struggles are manageable. I like to say that **every day is a battle, so every**

day we prepare for war. We are not perfect, but we try to move a little closer to perfection every day. Our family WILL live happily ever after, and **I am thankful!**

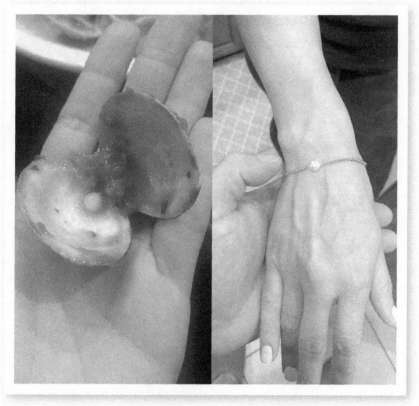

God's wedding present, the pearl that we discovered on the night of our marriage.

I've been places that most people will never visit, and I've had the fortune and misfortune of experiencing the highs and lows of life, love, and brutally violent combat. When I reflect back on this journey, I realize that it was the people I met along the way who were important. Those who I encountered in this life shaped who I am. My parents, Mr. Murphy, Coach Lyons, Drill Instructor

Martinez, my command master chief, Jason Workman, and my children all made me a better man. I don't think any of them, except maybe for DI Martinez in the sand pit, influenced me consciously—they just did the right thing and set the example. I hope that everyone reading this, and especially my children, will remember that. Live life like someone is watching, because they are.

I exchanged my body armor for my beautiful wife, Amanda.

HOT WASH

Drop the walls and open up your heart. I've lived and worked with the toughest men alive. I've jumped out of planes; I've had our enemies' blood splattered on my boots; and I've worn the uniform of our nation with pride. I've bonded with other men in ways that few others will ever experience. I see a lot of guys out there wanting you to think they are cool because they were in special operations or look a certain way. I've been guilty of it myself. The reality, though, is that **there is nothing more manly or cool than being there for those who you love**. At the end of the day, my family doesn't care how many bad guys I killed, how big my biceps are, or how many followers I have. All that matters to them is that I am present, committed, and engaged in their lives.

Nothing beats the awesomeness of humanity and family. I will leave you with a quote that gives me constant inspiration:

People travel to wonder at the height of the mountains, at the huge waves of the seas, at the long course of the rivers, at the vast compass of the ocean, at the circular motion of the stars, and yet they pass by themselves without wondering.

—St. Augustine

We are beautifully made.

Passion & Purpose

ACKNOWLEDGMENTS

I'd like to thank everyone who made the telling of this story possible. It all started when **Paul Cooper,** my pastor at Encounter Church in Broken Arrow, Oklahoma, encouraged me to put my experiences on paper and later provided fantastic feedback. **Paul,** thank you for showing me what it means to be a warrior for Christ. You have a beautiful gift and a heart on fire for Christ!

Those words sat on the shelf for years until fellow-SEAL **Mike Ritland** had me on as a guest on his *Mike Drop* podcast. Telling my life story out loud and receiving the response that I did made me realize that there was an appetite for a book on the subject. That podcast episode ultimately became the outline for *Unafraid.*

The next step was reaching out to my friend and co-writer, **Keith Wood**. I could not have asked for a more talented writer than you. Thank you for taking my story and making it come alive. You are gifted, hard-working, trustworthy, and, most importantly, my close friend. We have many more projects to do!

Many thanks to our agent, **Stephanie Cabot,** for all of your insight, support, and wisdom along the way. I'd also like to thank everyone at the **Scribe Publishing** team. Your dedicated and professional approach helped make this book what it is. You are the best around at what you do.

Thanks to **Lt. Col. J.B. Marshall**, USAF, (Ret.) for the idea to synch each chapter's lessons learned with the "Hot Wash" theme. Thanks also to everyone who read early drafts of this manuscript and offered your invaluable input. You know who you are.

Zach, thank you for all of the help on the book cover design and for always sticking good ink into my skin. More tats to come!

Dom Raso, you saved me on more than one occasion, my friend. I couldn't have asked for a better teammate to take it to the enemy and CRUSH anything and everything in our way.

Joe, we were the only two to stay roommates all the way through BUD/S. I don't believe in coincidences, but iron does sharpen iron. You are iron!

Forrest Lindekens, your selflessness and wisdom are unmatched. You are a true friend.

True North Ministry, your organization reaches so many men, and I'm glad to have been one. Don't ever stop doing what you are doing; you are life changers.

To the **Laverty Lane Crew,** we were kids, but man did we have a blast. Thank you to all of my childhood friends who were just as nuts as I was. Those memories are forever in my brain.

John Eldridge and the Wild at Heart team, you guide men into becoming men! This is needed in the world more than anything. Thank you!

To **the families of my fallen brothers**: your husbands, fathers, sons, brothers, nephews, and cousins will never be forgotten. They made the rest of us better, and I thank God every day for the time that I was able to spend with them. I sincerely hope that I did their lives and legacies justice in this book.

To my extended family, **Christa, Chad, Annette, Judy, Mark, Brandon, and kiddos**: We are not a big family, we *are* a family, and I wouldn't have it any other way. Thank you all for influencing me and always being there for support. Our holiday gatherings are always the best of times. I love you all!

Mom, you did a kick-ass job of raising me on your own. You set a great example for me, and I have tremendous respect for how hard you struggled to do your best for me. You were always there when I needed you: in my childhood, throughout my military career, and when I became a father. You stepped up as a grandmother when I needed you most—we might have all drowned without you. You have been *the* constant source of strength and peace in my life.

Dad, you taught me two really important lessons: be honest, and get things done. You diving out of the boat in Tennessee to retrieve the lost anchor is the perfect example of who you are and how you influenced me. You helped shape both my mindset and my work ethic. You also led by example when it came to personal fitness— you're still a stud. Boys can spend their entire life in search of their father's approval; I know that I have yours and that you are very proud. This warms my heart like you could not believe. Thank you!

As you may have guessed by now, my children mean the world to me. **Kailha**, you are Daddy's little girl. When you crawled onto my chest during BUD/S, you may have thought that I was comforting you; the reality is that you were comforting me. No child should ever have to step into the motherhood role the way that you did, and I thank you for it. I know it was hard, but I also recognize that it helped shape you into the amazing person that you are today. To see you become the woman and mother that you have become swells me up with pride.

Samantha, you are my little athlete with a huge heart. You were the greatest big sister imaginable for Triston. When I was emotionally unavailable, you stepped up and made sure that his childhood did not suffer. Your kind heart brought warmth and stability to our home, and your willingness to always help out made my job as a father possible. I'd like to take credit for your determined and "can do" attitude, but it's all you.

Triston, the fact that I had the privilege of raising you since you were a ten-month-old has built an unimaginable bond. You are my little buddy, no matter how big you get. I love your smile, your one-liners, and your always-positive approach to life. You have the palate of a food critic, and I love tasting your latest culinary creations.

Rick, my stepdad. Thank you for the endless love and support to my mother and to the rest of the family. There is never a dull moment with you two!

To my stepmom, **Carol**, you are a kind and genuine woman. I'm thankful that my dad found his partner in crime.

My father-in-law, **Rick Rose**, Army Special Forces, Vietnam. RIP. We never got the chance to meet sir, but the stories that I've been told reveal that you were truly a warrior for good. Your daughter carries that fighting spirit within her.

My mother-in-law, **Bonnie**, you raised a wonderful, caring, beautiful woman. You have been through a great deal and your strength shines through.

To my stepdaughter, **Emma**, you have all the smarts, kid. Allow that amazing brain to run to its potential and make this world a better place.

My stepson, **Brayden**. Hey wild man, don't ever change! Use your energy for good!

To my wife, **Amanda**, meeting you was the greatest thing that's ever happened to me. I questioned some of my past life decisions but, in the end, they led me to Texas and into your arms. I've been to the dark side of life, and you inspire me to do better, to be better. It's not always going to be smooth sailing, but with you by my side, I know we can continue on our path of happiness. We are far stronger together than either of us would be apart. You are my girl, and I love you more than anything. You are also really, really hot.

And last, but most certainly not least, **God**—You are my rock! Even though I may stumble, You never allow me to fail. I love You!

ABOUT THE AUTHORS

Eddie Penney spent twenty years in the US military, first as a Marine Infantryman and a Navy SEAL. Eddie completed seven combat deployments during the Global War on Terror, five of them with the Navy's most elite unit. He completed hundreds of high-risk missions as both an assaulter and breacher. He now serves as the founder and CEO of Contingent Group, a private security firm specializing in international operations. Eddie is also a motivational speaker, mentor, and founder of the UNAFRAID brand. He lives in the Dallas area with his wife, Amanda, and their five children Kailha, Samantha, Triston, Emma, and Brayden.

Keith Wood partnered to write three novels, two of them *New York Times* Bestsellers, under the joint pseudonym "Jack Carr." Keith has written hundreds of feature articles for outdoor publications and is also an attorney. He lives in Alabama with his wife, Emily, and their three children Victoria, Elizabeth, and James.